the Starseed sacred circle

The Starseed Sacred Circle

A JOURNEY BACK TO YOUR TRUTH

YOLANDI BOSHOFF

Copyright © 2021 Yolandi Boshoff

All rights reserved. No part of this publication may be reproduced, distributed or transmitted in anyform or by any means without permission of the publisher, except in the case of brief quotations referencing the body of work and in accordance with copyright law.

The information given in this book should not be treated as a substitute for professional medical advice; always consult a medical practitioner. Any use of information in this book is at the reader's discretion and risk. Neither the author nor the publisher can be held responsible for any loss, claim or damage arising out of the use, or misuse, of the suggestions made, the failure to take medical advice of for any material on third party websites.

978-1-913590-26-0 Ebook
978-1-913590-25-3 Paperback

The Unbound Press
www.theunboundpress.com

Hey unbound one!

Welcome to this magical book brought to you by The Unbound Press.

At The Unbound Press we believe that when women write freely from the fullest expression of who they are, it can't help but activate a feeling of deep connection and transformation in others. When we come together, we become more and we're changing the world, one book at a time!

This book has been carefully crafted by both the contributors and publisher with the intention of inspiring you to move ever more deeply into who you truly are.

We hope that this book helps you to connect with your Unbound Self and that you feel called to pass it on to others who want to live a more fully expressed life.

With much love,
Nicola Humber

Founder of The Unbound Press
www.theunboundpress.com

CONTENTS

INTRODUCTION   i

HERSTORY

THE BEGINNING	1
AKASHIC RECORDS	9
STARSEEDS	13
Starseed groups	20
THE GRIDS	29
THE STARSEED WOUND	35
SPIRITUAL BYPASSING	43
Focusing on the positive	44
Hierarchy	49
Over reliance on your guides	56
Victim of your sensitivity	58
Ascension obsession	60
Allowed	64
My Responsibility	67
LIGHT LANGUAGE	69
DNA ACTIVATION	77
THE PATRIARCHY	87
My Take	92
The Persecuted	98

The Persecutor	102
My Choice	106
SOUL-LED REVOLUTION	109

THE JOURNEY

THE STARSEED SACRED CIRCLE	121
THE NORTH	125
Mother Gaia	127
The Shadow Desire	128
The North Meditation	131
Shadow Desire Clarity	132
THE EAST	139
Andromedan Energies	141
Finding Your Truth	142
The East Meditation	146
Questioning Your Truth	147
THE SOUTH	151
Sirius Energies	153
Observation	155
The South Meditation	160
Expectations	160
The Healing Journey	164
THE WEST	167
Pleiadian Energies	172
Power Play	174

The West Meditation	178
Embodiment	179
Fearless	181
THE CENTER	185
Arcturian Energies	187
Trust	190
The Center Meditation	195
Your Treasure Chest	195
Overwhelm	197
NOW WHAT?	201

IN CLOSING

MAGIC	209
EPILOGUE	215
ACKNOWLEDGEMENTS	219
ABOUT THE AUTHOR	223

INTRODUCTION

As you start to read this book please know this - this is my truth.

I have taken a lot of time to work through my beliefs, my shadows, my fears, my filters and my opinions. What I share in this book is my truth. I stand behind it, BUT I am also very aware and have seen in my own spiritual evolution how our thoughts, ideas and truths grow, expand and change.

So, I implore you to read it all but only take what resonates with you. We will be working with finding your truth, uncovering it and how to own it. So, make sure you focus on always feeling into your own being. What are you feeling or sensing whilst reading the words? What does your body feel like?

My goal with all my work and my words is to steer you ever closer to your Soul. And if you are not sure what that is or if you think your truth needs some refining then I welcome you on this journey with me. I am hoping through sharing my truth it will guide you closer to your own truth.

Through my journey I have taken various truths and put them into my treasure chest of knowledge. Other bits I have thrown out and redefined. There is no right or wrong. There is only how you feel within.

In this book I wanted to share more of my own personal experiences with you in the HerStory section. Here I share what I have learnt over the years and how my journey unfolded with the Akashic Records, Light Language, Starseeds, Earth Energy and DNA Activation. Showing you how we are really all connected to the gorgeous energies of the Universe and that in essence we are all born into this incarnation with all the beautiful gifts right at our fingertips.

Through my own journey I then developed the Starseed Sacred Circle process and I share this in The Journey section of the book. This is a time of deep introspection, moving through your fears and judgement, and reconnecting with your authentic self. The insights, questions and meditations that I share there, are all connected to the different Star groups that I work with and with Mother Gaia. Take your time to sit with the information and start delving deeper into who you are as a person in this now life.

I designed this whole process so you can understand yourself, your ideas and your truth again. For too long we have been in acceptance of what we have been told.

Our Souls are crying out for us to remember again.

So join me in a journey of re-membering. Allow yourself to let go and tune into the magic of who you are.

Much love Yolandi

HERSTORY

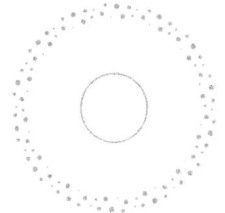

THE BEGINNING

It is always hard to know where to start when you speak about a journey, but I guess the beginning is as good a place as any. This journey led me to creating what is now known as the Starseed Sacred Circle and I would like to share this with you, as this work has impacted my life and those clients who dared to go deeper within themselves.

So much has unfolded and transpired over this time, but this was the beginning of my soul journey. The beginning was about making a choice. A choice to step into the unknown. A choice to start listening to my Soul.

The beginning…

I opened my email and there it was, a message from my boss apologising to say that the company can't renew my business analyst consultancy for the next year. My heart stopped; my reality crumbled as I sat there staring at the screen. I did not know what to do. My world fell apart.

I had the perfect life, working from home in South Africa, three to four days a week, paid in Pounds Sterling and a very flexible job for an international company. Sure, there was a lot of late nights, but it was a pretty amazing gig and no commuting to work each day. Comfy at my work desk starting work at 9 am each day, what more could a girl ask for!

Looking back at that particular moment, I can see now how the purpose in my life just disappeared. I was defined by my job and my income and in one email all this was pulled away from me. I was left in a blank, void space of nothingness.

This was a defining moment in my life. I had to make a decision. I had to choose my way of being from this point forward….

And I had no clue. I did not understand the concept of being guided by my Higher Self or even Guides or Angels. It was me, myself and I sitting at that desk all alone. Life stopped.

Earlier that same year, 2014, I had my Akashic Records read. Now if you have never heard of the Records before, let me give you a quick rundown. The Akashic Records is like a massive database or library. In this library there is a book for every Soul that has ever been or will ever be. Souls all have their own book with information about their past, present and future. Everything you have ever thought, felt, done, all neatly kept in this energetic database or library. And the best part – we are all able to access this database and information about ourselves, other Souls, events and places around the whole Universe. Everything that has ever happened is energetically available to us to access. Now at the time of having my own Akashic Records read I knew nothing about what I just told you. I was so beautifully naïve that I assumed the lady reading them was a well-trained psychic with the ability to access my Past Life information. I did not even understand the concept of the energy that we could all access and connect with.

And then as she started my session, she asked if I knew that I was a healer?

As a staunch businesswoman working in a corporate environment for many years, I wasn't 100% sure about her statement, but my brain started connecting the dots. I was a professional business analyst after all?

As a person who thought about studying psychology many years ago this sort of made sense. I gave up on completing my studies, as all the rules and regulations about how the human worked freaked me out and I hated the structure and boxes they wanted to apply to our behaviour, so I quit. At work, I was the go-to person for people with issues, a great listener, and a soft heart to boot. Everyone loved to talk to me about their problems, and my advice was pretty much respected too. I also started and ran the Corporate Social Responsibility project for one of my previous companies, I was always involved in some sort of charitable work. So, I guess helping people was something I was into….

Amazing what happens when we start to put it all together and realise where some of our gifts lie.

The word 'healer' was such a broad term, and for my mind and consciousness at that stage, the closest thing to what I understood would have been Reiki. I did not actually realise that a healer meant so many things and that the energy of the healer is really about being with people and holding space.

Technically, this could mean working as a manager in a corporate environment or being a therapist or even a teacher.

Living at that stage totally in my masculine energy, the first step after finding out that I am a healer was obviously to study to be a healer. And the one healer I knew was my amazing Reiki massage therapist. I insisted that she trained me in Reiki Level 1 and 2, so within six months I was a qualified Reiki practitioner. Right, job done Universe, I am now officially a healer but still working as a business analyst on the side. I could totally juggle this – three to four days of creating amazing apps for the Financial Industry and one to two days of healing work – surely this is what dreams are made of?

Soul purpose fulfilled!

But no, the Universe had a different idea – let's take away the biggest part of Yolandi's existence and see what she chooses. The Universe and the Soul demanded my full commitment to this concept.

By pulling my cushy job from under my butt and leaving me high and dry I would be forced to take a stand – to choose a side!

That month I evaluated all my options. I was working for a UK based company doing my consultancy work remotely in South Africa four days a week. It was the best job ever, lots of flexibility, lots of money and lots of time to also spend with my little boy. But now, if I chose to stay in corporate, I would have to commute for at least 2.5 hours a day into Cape Town, almost the same amount of money but a lot less time with my family and a lot more stress. (This was all happening in the time before the world realised that working remotely was a great idea).

It just did not feel right and no other consultancy jobs working from home were panning out. So, I sat down with the husband and we spoke about the situation. I was wondering if pursuing a career as a Reiki healer might be a full-time option for me…

He was super supportive and made it clear that this was my choice. At that stage, our son was still young, and I wanted to be there for school pick up and to spend more time with him, so working in the city just didn't feel right. I took the decision and chose the path of a healer.

This path was riddled with doubt and fears, but I just had to try, right?

I jumped in, sending out emails to everyone stating that I was now a Reiki healer, practicing on friends and family, printing flyers, and leaving them everywhere I could think of. But it was crickets, no phone calls, no bookings, nothing was happening. It was crazy, I was feeling so lost at that point in time. I showed up and I tried everything I knew but obviously there was something amiss.

A month later my friend invited me to a two-day session in beautiful Hermanus with an amazing Shamanic Healer. It was so incredible, two days of going deeper, looking at what my Soul wanted to do. Clearly for the first time seeing all my fears and insecurities about being a healer. I had these ideas held within me about how I thought things should be and now seeing so visibly in this workshop that I had no control over any of what was happening. I had to learn to trust the signs, not just be in my masculine-doing energy of control and action. And then on the last day during our very last meditation I got a clear message. I went into this meditation and ended up in a large cave with a very old Bushman. When I looked into his eyes it felt like I was looking into my own eyes. We sat down in the cave around the fire and my message was to work with the Akashic Records. Inside in my heart I knew that this felt right. There was something there and I needed to go and look. The next big step was happening, and I needed to listen.

I hadn't really thought about the Akashic Records and literally did not even know where to start. Then as I got home that evening and I opened my email there was a message about a course running and a special offer for the next 24 hours. My heart skipped a beat and I thought, 'You better listen', and there and then I bought the online course. The signs were showing themselves to me and I had a choice – listen or overthink.

I started studying the next week and that was the beginning of my journey as a healer. I did also finish my Reiki Masters later that year, with another teacher that broadened my horizons even further and this connected me with one of my dearest Soul Sisters who has been walking by my side ever since.

AKASHIC RECORDS

And so my journey towards myself and going deeper started to unfold.

I spent five years reading the Akashic Records for hundreds and hundreds of clients. It became very clear to me that my talent for being a business analyst could be utilised in the energy realms of the Universe. My skills to put things together and see patterns and come up with solutions could be utilised in this work as well. I merged my business skills with my newfound woo skills and created a beautifully successful business. One thing I am still helping my clients with to this day is how to live in this 3rd dimensional (3D) expression of being human, running a business and utilising our psychic and healer skills together.

Working with the Akashic Records taught me how to trust my inner knowing. It showed me that everything we feel and experience whilst connecting with the energy out there is relevant and has a place.

Initially, when I started this work it was all about understanding Past Lives and seeing how those blocks created in those lives energetically showed up again in this lifetime. If I chose to give up my power in a previous life, I would definitely be confronted by the same scenario in this lifetime. And through this understanding, I could start to find the patterns in the lives of my clients and see how they repeatedly kept on following the same story. This work was very powerful and helped so many to see where they were stuck. But as I evolved as a spiritual being, I also realised that there was way more to the Akashic Records than just the bad stuff we created. There was this ability for us to see our own potential. There was this space where the Soul wanted to speak about what it likes to do, things that make it happy and feel fulfilled. I started investigating what I call positive Past Lives. And it was so magical, the things I saw and could share with my clients gave them a lot more clarity on where they could go and step more solidly into their purpose. There my business started to take a turn – I was putting my attention more on what I could create vs what I created in the past. I loved it! I loved seeing the potential unfold and the happiness of people stepping back into who they want to be at a Soul level.

I also started realising that I could connect to places, timelines, and events in the Akashic Records and this filled me with even more excitement. This magical energetic space held so many answers for us all to explore.

Doing this work made me realise that we all have access to this field of information. You do not need to be special or a born mystic. All humans can access this field of energy – you just need to learn how.

I knew that my Soul wanted me to help people realise that they are filled with so much more potential than they ever realised. I was actually so grateful for the fact that I wasn't born psychic or had experiences of seeing Spirit as a child. I was shown that you can learn to be psychic and to understand and work with energy from any age. I only started at the age of 37, so surely if I could do this, anyone could. It literally just took a lot of practice and belief and you can make it happen.

I proceeded to teach others how to access the Records. I wanted to get rid of the myth around some people being more spiritual and special than others and that is why they could do this work. Everyone has a right to look at the information. It is there for us all to use, to investigate, to learn and to expand our consciousness.

It just takes commitment!

The more we open our hearts, let go of our restrictive beliefs and ideas, the more we get to connect with the information held in this energy field. I do also believe that some psychics will be better than others. It's a bit like learning to sing vs having a talent from birth. Beyoncé vs Yolandi on the singing front will be a vast difference. But if I kept on practicing every day I would get pretty amazing at singing. It all depends on my level of self-belief and commitment. We as humans can make literally anything happen for ourselves. We just need to believe that it is possible. And me, forever seeing possibilities in all of humanity, truly believe that we are all capable of creating something amazing in our lives.

STARSEEDS

I am guessing when you picked up my book and looked at the title with the word Starseed, you knew something about it or you must have heard something about the term. Allow me to share my version of being a Starseed and how I work with this knowledge.

All those years back when the lady did my Akashic Record reading she also mentioned another pivotal thing that changed my life even more. She mentioned that I was a Mission Realmer connected to the Andromeda Galaxy. Mission Realmers are from the angelic dimension linked to Andromeda.

As she spoke those words, I burst into tears. Deep inside me it all felt right! I knew it to be my truth. I had never even heard of Starseeds, I did not even understand the concept, but my whole being welcomed these words.

It all made sense, my uncomfortableness around being on Earth, always being dubbed the weird one. I pushed all the weirdness down to fit into the corporate mould after school, to make sure that I performed and fitted into this world.

So there and then I was given my explanation and a ticket to own my weirdness again!

Here is my take on the concept:

When we are sparked by the Divine (Source, God whatever term you like to use or believe in), our Souls choose to incarnate somewhere first. Some Souls choose to come to Earth as part of their first incarnation, other Souls choose to go to another planet, realm or dimension first. Our Souls also love to travel around, spend time around the Universe and learn new things. So even if you were incarnated somewhere first, you might have spent time in many other places before you came here.

There are many, many different groups of Starseeds out there and in my work I have dealt with more than 20 different groups, but each day, I am still learning more. New groups are being revealed as we speak. The majority of Souls here on Earth are what we call Earthseeds. These are Souls that are very comfortable here, this is their first place of incarnation. They are connected to Mother Gaia and happy to be here and live their life on this plane. Many of them also connect and understand the bigger picture of being on this Earth and loving and working with her.

I always describe being a Starseed like this – I am South African, I was born there but I have lived in various other countries during my life – Namibia, Germany and England. Every time I move to another country, I take on some of their traits, traditions and ideas. I love German traditions and speaking German. In England I love the countryside, old traditions and history. So, I make those part of my life even though I am South African.

So as an original Mission Realmer, I know I have spent time on a load of other planets – I have a very deep connection with the Pleiades, Sirius and Arcturus. I have learnt things from being there and have put that information in my spiritual toolbox and use it in my work and life here now on Earth.

Eventually, once my Soul felt ready, I decided to come here to Earth to do some more work here and learn more about being in this dense 3D reality. The choice to come to Earth is an interesting one as this is a unique experience. Here you can combine the spiritual, mental and emotional aspects of being. You get to feel emotions and connect with an instinctive ego that wants to keep you safe and in survival mode, whilst trying to live in that spiritual realm as well. Talk about a freaking mind-blowing experience! Wouldn't you also want to come here?

BUT one of the biggest issues for all Starseeds incarnating here is to try and combine all these parts together. To reach that point of connection with Mother Earth and feeling like I belonged took a lot of hard work and deep Soul searching. 2018 was the first year that I really started connecting with Mother Earth.

Before then I was all up in the Cosmos, working with the Star energies and having a great time connecting with all the energies out there. But then in 2018 my physical body started asking for earth connection. I woke up one day and had this intense need to go to Peru. I had no idea why I had to go there, but it felt so important that I just had to follow my instinct. I booked a 20-day trip all by myself and off I went.

During this time, I joined a couple of retreats but spent a lot of time alone which was an interesting experience. When I was in Cusco, one of the people I met suggested that I try and get hold of this Shaman who could take me around Saqsaywaman (a massive stone settlement above the town). I messaged him the day I arrived and miraculously he had the next day open before starting work with another group. He could take me around the site and show me what was happening there.

It was an incredible experience and when he took me to a massive stone connected to the great wall, he asked me to connect my forehead to this ancient stone and he started chanting behind me. I stood there for a few minutes, he then asked me to move to another stone and stand with my back against the stone and then close my eyes and just breathe. I had no idea what was happening, but I stood there and just felt my breath deepening and then my arms started feeling very light and all I wanted to do was lift my arms in rhythm with the breaths I was taking. And then as I stood there, I realised what I was feeling was the rhythm and breath of Mother Gaia. I could feel her breathing. I burst into tears as I realised that he was showing me that she was alive and that we could feel her. It was such an incredible experience, and I am still so grateful to this man for opening up my eyes and my being to Mother Gaia.

As 2018 continued, my Peruvian experience was a beautiful reminder of our connection with the Earth, but I was still feeling uncomfortable being here and I was in a lot of resistance. I then joined another retreat to some incredible sacred sites in South Africa later that year. We visited the beautiful moon landscape near Kaapsehoop a gorgeous little town in Mpumalanga province. We were there for an early morning meditation and as we got to the edge of the cliff there was this amazing rock sticking out of the cliff and in front of us was a blanket of clouds. It was beautiful and it felt like I was standing at the edge of the world.

As I got my turn to sit and meditate on this big rock, I was overcome with this longing to go home to Andromeda, to leave this earth and just return to being up there in the Stars. I was crying so much as I sat there, but inside of me a voice said, 'Put your hands on the rock'. As I did this, I heard the voice of Mother Earth. She asked me if I remembered why I came here.

Did I remember that I asked to come here and do my work?

Did I remember that I wanted all of this?

My world stopped. I asked for this, I wanted this, I CHOSE THIS…

Right there and then I realised that I needed to stay and show up. My Soul wanted to be here; she made the decision to shine her light on this planet. Not back home in the Stars, but right here and right now, she wanted to be seen and to serve and to help. That day I chose to stay and work as the Lightworker Starseed that I am.

So, if you are feeling the pull, if you know deep inside that you are also a Starseed, know also that you and your Soul chose to come here and do the work.

You chose to come and expand your consciousness and the consciousness of those around you. You chose to come and share the love and light within with those around you.

You also came here to experience the full range of human emotions – fear, anger, hate, love, joy, shame, guilt, obligation, suffering, bliss, pride, regret, pain, peace and compassion. You came here to be in light but also to be here in darkness.

This experience is one of a kind. It is unique and incredible, so treat it as such.

After my beautiful Mother Earth connection, my work really started to shift. My intuitive abilities expanded, and I started to understand that in order for me to expand my consciousness and my connection to the Star Beings out there that I loved so much I needed to be fully grounded and rooted here on this planet.

STARSEED GROUPS

There are a multitude of different Starseed Groups out there as I have mentioned before, and so many that are still coming forward as well. I will share some of the ones that I have worked with over the years and some of the general traits of them. Please note that there are many other groups out there that I have not yet worked with or mentioned here.

There is loads of information on the Internet and there are amazing people out there channelling information about Starseeds. I personally have learnt a lot from so many amazing channelers and teachers out there including Susann Taylor Shier, Celia Fenn, Andrea Hess, Steve Nobel and then of course my Guides and my Soul.

Always make sure that when you read something, that you tune into your body and see how it feels for you. You will know if something is right for you or not. So please remember this if you decide to do some more research on Starseed Groups. As with everything, we all carry our own truth.

Being able to determine where you originate from is a bit of a tricky concept as often different people will come up with different groups for an individual and again this has a lot to do with where you have been before and how much of their traits you work with or take on.

There is nothing set in stone around finding your group, it is very much about what feels good to you. Like I mentioned before I have my main group, the Mission Realmers of Andromeda that I feel extremely connected to, but then I work with the Pleiadians, Arcturians and Sirius groups all the time as well.

You can go to a person who works with Starseed energies and get a reading done or you can always see what feels good to you. So as you read this list below – take a few deep breaths in, set the intention to connect with a group that you have worked with before and then as you read through the list pay attention to what your body is guiding you to.

Here are a few groups with a short overview of each. I go more into depth about the Andromedans, Sirius, Pleiadians and Arcturians later in the book.

ANDROMEDANS

>They are all about finding freedom.
>They are avid spiritual seekers and teachers.
>They are connected to the emergence of the Divine Feminine.
>More info on them in the East section of the book.

SIRIUS

>They are deeply connected to the ancients.
>They love to make things better.

They represent the balance between the masculine and feminine energies.

More info on them in The South section of the book.

PLEIADIANS

They are here to assist the world with changes.

They inspire us to get things done.

Visionaries and the rebels among us.

They love building communities.

More info on them in The West section of the book.

ARCTURIANS

They embody spiritual wisdom and consciousness.

They are here to share their insight with the world.

They are the influencers behind influencers, always working in the background inspiring others with their insight.

More info on them in The Center section of the book.

ALPHA CENTAURI

They help us move beyond negativity.
They know that the Source lives within us all.
They are extremely practical and hardworking.
They are often workaholics.

HADARIANS

They come from a planet of unconditional love, that was destroyed.
They are here bringing love to the planet.
They often struggle with co-dependency and victimhood. Very powerful if they transcend this energy.

LYRANS

They are the oldest Souls we know of.
They were responsible for the seeding of various other Star systems.
They are extremely intelligent, hold deep spiritual wisdom and knowledge and leadership skills.

MALDEK

They blew up their own planet, so very worried about messing up in this life.
They love to overthink things.
They are amazing strategists and analysts, able to create real magic.

MINTAKANS

They are from a beautiful water planet that they had to leave.
They light up the world and see the potential in others beautifully.
They are the networkers amongst lightworkers.

MISSION REALMERS

They are here to resolve negativity.
They are from the angelic realm of the Andromeda Galaxy.
They are here to bring light.

NIHAL

A lot of Indigo and Crystal children come from here.

They are all about questioning society and our old ways.
They are extremely innovative and creative.
Here to change the world.

ORION

They are all about finding spiritual truths.
They are driven by knowledge and ask so many questions.
They are very energetically sensitive.

POLARIS

They are working towards ascension and the big shift we are experiencing.
They are all about oneness and unity. They are all about moving out of polarity.
They are a true north for many and deeply connected to the Earth.

PROCYAN

They are all about sunshine.
They bring joy to the world.
They are learning to overcome the dualistic view of body and Soul.

SPICA

They are here to help us towards enlightenment.
They need nature to function on this planet.
They bring neutrality and clarity to the planet.

VEGA

They are bright shining lights.
They are extreme fun and bring so much laughter to the world.
They need a stage to perform and entertain the world.

This should give you a general idea of what we are dealing with when we speak about being a Starseed. If any of these deeply resonated with you then make an effort to investigate them further. I always feel that Starseed Souls are really here to help humanity and the planet and that they carry a lot of knowledge and wisdom with them, but Earthseed Souls have a deep connection to this planet and the wisdom that she carries and we all can learn so much from each other.

And always remember that this is only one part of who we are, we are still human having this earthly experience too. So that fact unites us all and the planet on a very deep level.

THE GRIDS

Imagine a great big web woven around Mother Earth. In every single section of the web, where the lines of the web meet, a person is standing. A bit like little antennas that connect all the lines of the web. Each person has a section of the web that they are connected to and their energy also connects them to other little antennas around the web. This beautiful grid is also connected to Mother Earth and we share energy with her through this grid.

If I am properly stable and rooted into Mother Earth, my capacity to receive light and information is heightened. As a Starseed Lightworker I am here to bring love and light to this planet, but I can only do that by being in acceptance of being here. I am meant to receive various light codes from different light beings and planets, and I can only properly let these in if I am rooted to Earth. It is a bit like a magnet attracting the metal shavings on a big table. The stronger the magnet the more shavings it pulls towards it. The same with light codes, the more I shine, the more I attract.

The light codes that are being sent to us from various places within the Universe are important to help us unlock those parts of us that are needed here on Earth – those gifts that are locked within us. And as I consciously make time to receive these, I enable my gifts to be shared with those around me.

The light codes that I receive from the places throughout the Universe are also given to Mother Earth through the grid, and form part of her connection to the Cosmos as well. As she receives these light codes, she is also creating new energies within her own system and those in turn are then sent out to various of the antennas on the grid.

It is also important to know that there are various portals and places around the Earth that amplify this energy of receiving codes. Sacred Sites around the world help us to connect to certain energies out there in the Universe, they pull info from out there and if you step onto that site you receive those codes and energies within your light body.

What the Sacred Sites also do is they act like a repository for information. So ancient information is literally encoded into the energy of the site and when you step into it you can access that information. The ancient teachings and information are held right there for us all to look at, work with and share with the world. Also know that you can energetically connect with all Sacred Sites around the world and pull in info as required.

BUT we have forgotten all of this. Lucky for us, we are slowly remembering and opening ourselves up to this beautiful information again.

There are loads of other grids around the earth and we are all still learning to understand how they affect and work with our energies and those of the Earth and the Cosmos.

There is so much magic and potential out there that is just waiting for us to find it. The more we understand that we don't have to be caught in the hardship and heaviness of being here, the more we can see that we are actually built to receive magic. These bodies of ours are specifically designed to receive information through connection with energy. And energy is all around, every living thing on this planet carries energy. And you can read and interact and feel it all.

What I have also been shown is that certain parts of the web that is surrounding Mother Earth is dark. Some of the antennas that stand on those parts of the web have been corrupted by power and greed. And so I always have to be mindful of which parts of the web I consciously interact with. These antennas are receiving codes and information that is not for the highest good of humanity or Mother Earth. And therefore they are creating rotten patches in certain places.

Part of the work of lightworkers is also to become aware of these areas, shine a light on them and work towards the restoration of these parts. Some lightworkers are here to lead the revolution towards reclaiming those parts of the grid again and their work is to expose the darker side of our world and help the people that have been affected by it to heal from those experiences.

For me personally I always feel a great responsibility for keeping my little bit of the grid clean and healthy. Thus, my work is to constantly be checking in with myself, doing my shadow work and making sure that I am showing up in the best version of myself at that point in time. By me conducting my life from the energies of my woundings I am also projecting that onto those around me, so I always have to be very aware. I also feel that part of our journey here is to understand myself and my pain so I strive to cause less harm around me. The less I harm those around me and create wounds for them, the fewer wounded humans there are on the grid.

The Gridkeepers are the humans who are looking after the integrity of the grid. They are constantly working with different energies to repair and heal the grid and to make sure that the energy is flowing and receiving as it should. These gorgeous Souls literally make it their life mission to constantly work on these lines of energy within our world and to strengthen it too.

I have also been shown recently how a brand new grid is being created here on Earth by lightworkers all around the globe. This grid is connected to new frequencies coming in and new ways of thinking and feeling on this planet. The old structures and ways of working are slowly starting to fall away, as we have stepped into this new age of Aquarius. We are all being prepped for new ways of living and being on this beautiful planet.

There is also a lot that is not re-membered yet about the inner workings of Mother Gaia and how that affects and interacts with each of us here on this planet. She is consciously connected with each of us, and she also holds ancient information that again links to the Sacred Sites and other powerful vortex points around the Earth. As a collective, we are learning now how to work with her and use this information and I believe this is all part of the new age of Aquarius and how she is also ascending.

Sometimes I feel so overwhelmed by it all, but then I get filled with gratitude for the knowing that everything is indeed connected and part of everything else. We are connected to All that is…

THE STARSEED WOUND

The concept of the Starseed Wound hit me at 3 am one morning. I tend to have these weeks where my Soul and my Guides want to chat A LOT! I knew about the concept of the Witch Wounds, but I had never made the connection that I also carry Starseed Wounds. There is a lot of repressed trauma for the collective and especially Lightworkers around dying for their beliefs and truths and this is showing up now more than ever, ready for healing and release.

The concept of the Starseed Wound was shown to me as trauma around bringing light and consciousness back into the world. Many Starseeds spent lifetimes before coming to this planet, working to expand consciousness and fighting repression of the light. A lot of victim consciousness is locked deep within our cells and the realisation around this can be a life-changing experience.

I was also shown that our natural inclination as Lightworkers is to only talk about the light – holding onto false ideas about positivity and love and light. And the reason for this is our fear of the darkness. Deep within our own subconscious mind looking at the darkness and connecting with it again can result in death and trauma. So it makes it a lot easier to just be in the love and light and never actually confront our biggest fears and darkness within.

As a society, we have built an entire community around the concepts of love and light, bypassing responsibility for real life. We need to understand that we have to be in this real world, with real pain and suffering but also with real love and joy – learning to keep it real and not shame ourselves for experiencing humanness.

American psychologist and Buddhist practitioner, John Welwood came up with the term 'spiritual bypassing' in 1984. His observation was based on the behaviour of people to turn to spirituality to avoid dealing with painful emotions and challenges.

For many years, I have been looking at persecution of Lightworkers in my Past Life sessions with clients. The Witch Wounds run very deep in so many Lightworkers and this is one of the main reasons why it is so hard for many of us to show up and allow ourselves to be seen.

One can see the patterns of intense, unexplainable fear welling up in people. It is so debilitating, and it is truly a massive relief and healing experience to acknowledge and release this pain.

One thing that I always see in the Akashic Records with our Past Lives is how we often repeat certain stories or patterns. For a long time, I mostly delved into Lives here on this planet, but then when I was working with one of my own core shadows and a lot of pain in my solar plexus area I was taken out of my human timeline. To clarify, when I work with Past Lives I see the human experience as a long line. On this long energy line are all the Lives from this one going all the way back to your first incarnation on this planet. And I am then able to go to any of those Lives and start tapping into the story of that life.

I am aware of Parallel Lives, but in my visual brain that loves pictures, it is much easier to work with a concept of our Lives being run in a linear fashion. It also helps when you try and explain to clients what you are seeing.

I saw myself leaving the Earth Life line and then moving into a Before Earth Life line – a line filled with many lives and connections to different parts of the Universe.

I then had the experience of seeing a lifetime where I was not on the Earth and I was not a human being. I was in a great war with lots of other warriors behind me. We were fighting a legion of very dark and evil beings and I was leading a group. I remember looking back and saw some people that I knew behind me. As I turned forward a very big man walked straight up to me and stabbed me in my solar plexus area. I remember lying there watching everyone else dying and our mission fighting against the darkness failing, my heart broken.

The discovery of this lifetime was really hard for me as I personally knew those Soul faces behind me and I felt so responsible for being careless and so gung-ho about fighting these beings. My typical style of life is to run towards things that scare me but that is usually by myself. I don't drag others with me. So when I started my Soul business wanting to lead people back into the unknown and back to themselves I kept running into this self-imposed wall.

> Will I be dragging people back to their own demise?
>
> Can I hold myself responsible again for what happened back then?
>
> Could I be repeating this pattern of creating death for others in this lifetime?

Writing this now, I can see how crazy it might sound, but for me and many others, those feelings of intense fear are so real and it rules your life unless you work with this pain.

So many of us actually carry our Starseed Wounds into our human experiences. It is very important to be aware of these, as I have seen many clients working on Earth-related trauma for years and seeing no difference in their fear levels, but once we get out of this Earth timeline and back to their Starseed timeline we manage to heal those deep fears right at the start of their journey. It is also important to understand that some people don't necessarily have to go back to the Starseed timelines to heal, but healing might be needed on an Earth timeline level and it will achieve the same results.

The main thing with any of our Past Life wounds are that we have to find them, look at them and heal them. We carry a deep knowing within that there are unseen hurts that have to be released. So pay attention to what comes up and how you feel about parts of your journey. All these little clues matter so much.

And if you follow all the breadcrumbs, the bits and pieces that you discover, will eventually move you closer and closer to who you are and your sense of belonging within yourself.

I also wanted to add a little insight about Parallel Lives mentioned above. The Akashic Records hold all the possibilities of our choices within it, energetically. Every single choice that you make in your life has a path that leads from it and then from your next choice there is also a path and so forth and so forth. BUT all of your possible choices are shown in the Akashic Records even the ones that you haven't consciously taken. So let's say all those years back I chose not to become a healer and to continue my life as a business analyst. In my records, that choice point is there, and in the Records I can see how both paths play out. Consciously I am walking on the path of the healer now, but my life as a business analyst is still energetically there in the Akashic Records. It is still running and happening as we speak. The energy possibility is there…

This whole concept of the 'Garden of Forking Paths' is amazing and my mind struggles to comprehend and process it all and I am not sure we can ever fully explain or understand it. But again it is all energy and energy is filled with possibilities

SPIRITUAL BYPASSING

This concept forms the basis of a lot of what is happening in the world today. It is far easier for us to gloss over our wounds and put some ointment on the top, without actually looking at what the cause of our pain is. Somehow, we feel we can do some affirmations to talk ourselves out of our pain. Just think about it – you can try and convince your conscious mind, but at the end of the day there are issues deeper inside of you that you need to look at and heal.

Opening the door into that dark room is terrifying. The unknown of ourselves is such a scary thing, but we require courage. Speaking from experience – I cannot bypass my pain, it will come back to haunt me in some way, shape or form. It will keep on showing up until I take the bull by the horns, sit it down and look at it.

"Love and light is like butter on mouldy bread" – words from my gorgeous friend Lameze. I loved it when she said this during one of our many nature walks. I try and cover up the mould, the pain and the yucky bits. But at the end of the day the bread is still mouldy. I need to understand the issue, why is the bread mouldy?

I have a list of types of bypassing and want to share some of the examples here with you. I also want to share my own truth around these. I know, in the beginning of my journey, I have also dabbled in these concepts, but as I learnt more and understood my shadow more, I realised that they were just ways of superficially making myself feel better. Again, spreading the butter over that mouldy bread!

FOCUSING ON THE POSITIVE

Now this is a concept that I see a lot of in the world. Remember to be positive, everything is going to be okay as long as you look at the good in everything and everyone.

Well, guess what? Sometimes things are shit. Sometimes you are angry and frustrated and furious with good reason. And do you know what? It is okay to be angry. It is your right to be angry. You are allowed to be angry!

When you deny your right to be angry, you deny your right to be human. And the same for every other 'negative' emotion. Please note my inverted commas around the word negative. The world loves to brand things as positive or negative.

All emotions are valid – anger, guilt, frustration, impatience, grief, love, envy, sadness, anxiety, jealousy, joy – all of them! All emotions are energy.

Part of our 3D experience is being able to connect to different emotions. This is a unique Earth-centric capability. One of the reasons Souls choose to come here is to experience the emotional body in this dimension as it is not available anywhere else.

But somewhere a long, long time ago someone decided to create a distinction between emotions, placing judgement on emotion and labelling it good or bad. A bit like what happened in our society, but I will elaborate further on that in a later chapter on patriarchy.

We were also told that we are not to show or feel the bad emotions. Feeling emotions like jealousy, envy and anger is wrong. Thinking bad thoughts or feeling bad emotions will result in you burning in hell. Remember it's a sin! So what do I do, I swing the pendulum right to the other side and start telling myself that in order to survive, not die in the eternal flames of hell, I better make sure that I am all positive and love.

Completely denying myself the opportunity of learning from these amazing energies that I want to experience as a Soul. Our emotional bodies and energy fields were designed to deal with emotions. The emotions enter my system and then require to be felt. I am required to feel all the cells responding within my body to this emotion's energy. And then once fully felt, I allow it to be released again. I take from the emotions the lessons, the beauty and the learning.

But as I am still learning to understand this strange energy body, I sometimes get it wrong. I either take that emotion once it enters and I supress it into the depth of my being. I love to store anger in my liver and sadness in my heart. I hide it in my physical body and hold onto it in an unseen manner. It's a bit like sweeping things under the carpet, except I store it somewhere in my body.

Or once this emotion enters I like to hold onto it with my mental energy body. I find a space in my mind to keep this emotion of say, for instance, jealousy, and in those moments between living my life and being busy, like at night when I get into bed and want to fall asleep I start analysing it. I spend hours of my life looking at this emotion, over-analysing it, thinking about it over and over and over again. I am like a bulldog not wanting to let go of this piece of meat. Holding on and never wanting to let go, when instead my energy body was designed to feel it, work with it and then gently send it on its way out of my energy body again. Flowing in and out like water.

Our emotions are such beautiful teachers. They point us right at the resistance within ourselves. They show you truths, desires, wounds and love that you hold within you. They are sacred expressions that help us to become more conscious.

> What if anger was actually there to reconnect you with your sacred power?

What if jealousy was there to reconnect you with your creative abilities?

What if guilt was there to reconnect you with your compassion within?

What if frustration was there to help you change direction in your life?

What if impatience was there to help you learn to trust?

What if envy was there to propel you forward in a new way?

What if sadness was there to help you love yourself more?

What if anxiety was there to help you connect deeper with yourself?

If you allow yourself that moment in time to feel that emotion, you allow it to pass through your system. You can feel it, be in it and then take time to understand it. If every time that emotion arises you choose to push it down again into the depths of you it becomes bigger and bigger. And then one day you will feel a massive overwhelming explosion within when it gets too much. Something inside will break.

Allow yourself to feel it all. Allow yourself to also sit down with it and understand what triggered that emotion within you. Look at it and see what it wants to show you. The more you allow all your feelings to be real, happy and content will be showing up for you anyways. There will be more space within you for all feelings.

HIERARCHY

Often spiritual teachers, leaders and gurus are put on a pedestal by us. And sometimes they put themselves there as well.

But in reality, we are all equal. I might be one step ahead of you in my learning in one area of life, but you might be two steps ahead of me in another area of life. So why do we choose to elevate others?

Because we think, 'I don't trust myself enough. He or she will know the answer, they can guide me or give me the answers'.

So why don't I trust myself? In our lives, power is always shown as outside of us. We have been conditioned for centuries to believe that we have to go through someone or something to find our guidance. We are never at the top of hierarchy. We always have to have someone above us, to get wherever we want to go.

I have forgotten my connection to my own intuitive abilities. I have been taught that I need to listen to someone who is wiser and stronger than me. For so many centuries people have taken hold of power and wielded it over others. Told us that we are not capable of being powerful and magical all by ourselves. Because what would happen if Yolandi realised that she was an amazingly powerful being who could create her own destiny and change the world around her? Well, the powers that be would lose all control…

What if I told you that you can start teaching yourself to own your experience again, to trust yourself again. You can become the captain of your ship and sail wherever you feel you want to sail to. And the best way to do this is to listen to your body!

Yes, I do realise that we all need teachers to guide us closer to ourselves, but we need to use our bodies to choose teachers that are in alignment with our Soul and our needs. Often we choose teachers because we are feeling lost and directionless and desperate.

If you chose teachers who resonated with your energy and vibration and guided you to become the most beautiful version of yourself, how wonderful would that be?

Start at the beginning. Reconnect yourself again to your body and your own intuitive abilities, start listening to your body and following your instincts. Return to basics.

These are a list of what is known as our Clair senses – the natural abilities of our bodies to sense things. Our hidden psychic abilities that no-one wants to talk about in case we get burnt at the stake again. We stopped teaching ourselves how to connect to our bodies a long time ago and so many generations missed out on this magical ability because of fear of persecution. Our intuition was outlawed. We were forced to go through someone to get our guidance, but no more.

CLAIRVOYANCE

the ability to see clearly. You sometimes see flashes, visions, colours or signs pointing you to your truth.

CLAIRCOGNIZANCE

the ability to know. You have a feeling inside that you don't know where it comes from, but you know that something is true or false without being able to explain it.

CLAIRSENTIENCE

the ability to feel in your body. When you have goosebumps whilst talking about something or you feel uncomfortable in your stomach when you think about a person (gut feeling).

CLAIRAUDIENCE

> the ability to hear. You sometimes get a ringing in your ears that might confirm the truth or you might hear a song and the words will confirm a truth for you.

CLAIRGUSTANCE

> the ability to taste. You sometimes taste something that creates a memory that leads you to a truth that you hold.

CLAIRSALIENCE

> the ability to smell. As with the above ability you sometimes smell aromas that reminds you of memories or people.

You can take time to see which one of these intuitive abilities mentioned above resonates most with you. Then start using these abilities to make your choices in your life. If you need to, for instance, to make a decision about working with a person, close your eyes, take a few deep breaths and imagine them in front of you. Ask your Soul what you need to see. Then take time to tune into your body and see what it shows you. I believe the first thing that you experience/see/feel/hear is always your answer.

Our intuitive abilities are much faster than our brains' processing and thinking capabilities. So whenever you are presented with a choice, connect with the very first thing that comes up for you. That is your answer!

Your body is connected to your Soul. Your Soul is constantly speaking to you.

Becoming intuitive is like riding a bike. The more you do it the better you get at it. When I take myself as an example – 10 years ago, I literally did not even think about my intuition, in fact I was pretty useless at using it too, and I had no clue it was even a thing. Then when I started working with the Akashic Records, I had to practice my intuition every day, I had to tune into energy and trust what my body was telling me whilst I read the Records for others. So my intuition became stronger and stronger and stronger. Now it is seriously one of my superpowers and I can't live without listening to my body. So you are able to practice and get better, but you have to be committed to this path.

I obviously also take into consideration that there are natural psychics out there that were born with their intuitive abilities already in a pristine state and they are the amazing Souls who can connect with Spirit and energies from a very young age. But that wasn't my journey and so if you are reading this and not one of the lucky ones who walked into this incarnation already lit up, start practicing. I promise you it is a life changing experience being able to listen to your Soul.

Take what you need from your teachers around you but know that you are just as worthy and enlightened as anyone else.

Let's take responsibility for our paths and see how much influence we have over our choices and our trajectories. We have been gifted free will in this life experience, so let's use it wisely.

OVER RELIANCE ON YOUR GUIDES

So often you hear people speaking about how their Guides are showing them this or that. And I get that, been there done that and got the t-shirt.

BUT your Guides, Deities, Ascended Masters and Angels are not your voice. They are here to give us guidance or show us information through our journey. Again, they are teachers and guides, they are not higher on the ranking than your Soul.

Often we get so obsessed with their role in our lives that we forget to allow our Soul to lead. The journey is about learning to listen to your inner voice and not constantly relying on energies outside of yourself to make decisions for you.

The very first time I remember consciously tuning into my inner voice was during a call with a mentor of mine. I was so obsessed with my rigid way of reading the Akashic Records, connecting with the Guides and then asking them to show me the way.

She challenged me on the call to tell her what Starseed Group she was in. I was so freaked out, I usually had a whole ritual of finding out information before I saw clients, she wanted an answer right now. So, I took a deep breath in and I closed my eyes and tuned into my inner voice. I asked the question and went with the first word that came up for me. I told her that she was an Arcturian Starseed, she laughed out loud and said, 'That wasn't so hard now, was it?' Turned out it was correct and she had known this for many years. It was a big turning point for me. I was able to tune into my knowing then and started to let go of the rigid rituals that I was relying on.

I often feel like my Guides are parts of me that are showing up for me. When I see the beautiful warrior or shaman side of my Soul guiding me through situations it fills my heart. Those parts of me have been through situations like this in Past Lives, those parts of me know and have the wisdom ready to show me.

And yes, working with Angels, Masters and Deities or Star Beings is not wrong, but you have to learn that they are like assistants in our life. They are here to help out but not for you to hinge all your bets on them. They are not responsible for your journey; you and your Soul are here to learn to work together as a team.

VICTIM OF YOUR SENSITIVITY

This is such a common trait that I see amongst lightworkers. We forget that being sensitive is what all this work is about. And so often I find the most gorgeous lightworkers hiding themselves away from the world because they just feel too much. I know this is hard, but hear me out.

The fact that you have the ability and gift to feel what is happening with others and with the world around you is amazing. So many people feel nothing or really struggle to connect with feeling. Again, I am going to say that we all have the ability to feel and connect with energy, and if you are like me you will have to practice this, but it gets easier I promise.

The one thing that I love most about being sensitive or an empath, for those of you who identify with that term, is that I use this ALL the time in my work and interactions with people. The minute I tune into your energy I know what is going on and I can use this to guide or help you.

BUT the issue here is that sensitive people love to take on the issues of the whole world. So because I can feel it, I immediately think that it is my job to fix it or help in some way. This for me was an issue for many years until I realised that I needed to create boundaries between myself and the rest of the world. I literally can't fix everything that is wrong in the world, but I can choose where I want to use my gift. I am fully in charge of how and when I feel.

For me it was an ego issue. Because I knew what was happening and felt that I had the answer to help this person it was part of my calling to fix it. I eventually felt so drained and exhausted because I allowed myself to take on their pain and their issues. I would worry myself sick about everyone being okay and this literally brought me to my knees. So I had to make a change, become a hermit, stop the work that I so loved or learn to manage my energy and put some proper boundaries in place.

I always say to clients, the minute our session is done I have to close the door between us. I disconnect from their energy and literally visualise myself closing the door.

Healers often feel like it is their responsibility to make sure everyone is fixed. Healers are guides, they show you what you need to see and hear because they can feel your energy and understand it. Every person has a choice and if your client, friend, family member or loved one chooses to make a choice that is not Soul-aligned that is up to them. You cannot control what other people do with information, energy or guidance that you have provided for them.

Creating firm boundaries and understanding why I feel like I need to save everyone is really important. Healing those wounds will help you embrace being a sensitive. It will also set you free.

ASCENSION OBSESSION

Very often we use the idea of ascension and 5th dimensional (5D) interaction as a vehicle to escape our current lives. When things get tough instead of facing them head on, unravelling and dealing with it, we retreat into 5D land. So let me explain.

Ascension is basically the idea of rising up as part of our spiritual growth. You go through the process of developing your own self-awareness and this then facilitates the expansion of consciousness and connectedness.

3D is the level of consciousness of all humans on this planet. This is where we are right now, in the density of the planet, often connected to feelings of fear, separateness, lack and limitation.

5D or Yolandi-land as some of my friends call it, is what most people on their spiritual journey strive for. This is the spiritual dimension of connectedness, unconditional love, potential and the ability to take responsibility for our choices and our lives. It is the realm where there is so much potential and love available to all of us, where we have moved through fear and into owning our power.

We use our spiritual practices as a way to avoid doing the work to help ourselves and deal with this 3D reality that we find ourselves in. It is much easier to strive to be in 5D, connecting with all the epic potential but then to never actually deal with the pain, judgement and issues that are still binding you to this 3D reality.

Your Soul chose to come here to this Earth plane, to experience all that this place has to offer and as I have said before this includes all the emotions, pain, suffering, joy and love that you find here. Your mental and emotional bodies were designed for this experience. But they work together with your spiritual body. We don't have the concept of mind, body and soul for nothing. It shows us the unity that is available to us if we choose.

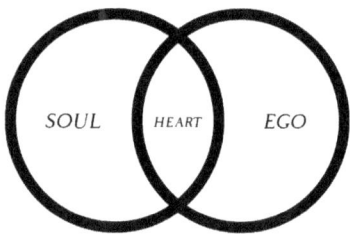

Imagine your Soul is the left circle and your Mind/Ego is the right circle, and these two parts are crucial to you being here on Earth. You cannot have this experience if you don't have both these elements within your body – Mind and Soul.

The little bit in the middle is the crossover – the point where our heart portal is. This is the place where our intuition sits, our guidance system. And it is perfectly positioned between the two most important parts of ourselves.

So this little portal part is what I use to navigate my life. I don't spend all my time in Soul or all my time in Ego/Mind. Balance is to recognise that I need to spend time in both of these parts of myself.

The ego experience is translated through the heart to the Soul. I need the higher Soul perspective on what I am experiencing in the Ego/Mind side of my life. And I get to listen to the Soul through the heart.

My heart/intuition or inner guidance system is how I hear my Soul's whispers and amazing ideas and concepts. I then take that through my heart and translate it to the Ego/Mind or the human side of myself.

But so many of us don't want to be responsible or connect with the human experience so we just stay in our heart and Soul space and completely ignore and turn our back on the Ego/Mind. Sitting around all day meditating and dreaming about how we wish the world to be vs actually getting our hands dirty and doing the work to create a new Earth.

Our constant need for ascending or fixing and healing and doing is negating the experience of being. The experience of being present and feeling and being here in this body on this Earth.

ALLOWED

I sat down a while back feeling very happy and grateful for what was unfolding in my life and inside of myself I was saying, 'The Universe allowed this'. And it hit me, like a ton of bricks, listen to what you are saying to yourself.

The Universe ALLOWED this….

That word struck me right in the heart. What??? How was I even thinking this, I know better than to allow outside forces to govern my existence and choices on this planet.

I then thought about something I said to myself many years ago about the husband allowing me to live my life the way I choose. Again, back then I had to stop myself from saying this, because he was not allowing me, he was supporting me in my choice to live my life a certain way.

This whole incident then led me back to my shadows. I was still needing to look at that part of me that feels I need permission and will be rewarded if I listen. Mic drop! Old patriarchal thinking right there. Going back to my church upbringing – if I am a good girl, the Lord will bless me.

But nothing that happens in my life is because I am a good or bad girl. Everything that happens in my life is governed by choices that I make and those then create circumstances. So as much as I might be imagining that the Universe is steering all of this there is a massive element of me being in control. Free will is a bit of a thing you know!

Every choice that I make to listen to my Soul is me aligning to the path that my Soul would love for me to follow. Her intention for me is always the highest good. Even if that path sometimes involves big lessons in my human eyes. She has an agenda, a tick list of things that she decided she wanted to engage with and learn. My choices on a human level tick off her list.

But I can very well decide not to, it just means that I might come back in another life to come and complete the tick list. And all of that is fine, I was given this Divine will of mine to use as I choose, so again no right or wrong.

I'm just on a mission here to see what would happen if I try to align as closely to that inner voice that keeps guiding me. I guess deep inside I am trying to prove the theory to myself that she is guiding me. And so far, the ride has been pretty epic, weird and insane. But it is fun too, so I choose to continue on this little trajectory of mine.

So back to you – where in your life do you feel someone, or something is allowing you to do something? And be honest with yourself here. This whole incident of me recognising that part of my internal talk was showing me how I still was not taking my power back 100%. That I was still giving it away to, in this case, 'The Universe'.

Being honest with yourself about what is being allowed is not always a nice place to be. But again, as part of me unravelling who I am, I need to understand my belief systems and see how they are serving me.

Often it is easier to put everything outside of myself because then I can't be responsible for the outcome. Responsible for failures or perceived failures. I walk around with so many ideas of how things should be presenting in my life and I am forever measuring myself against those. So, if I feel like I should be earning £10,000 per month and I am not, surely the Universe has decided not to bless me because I am a bad girl. But if I unravel why I want / need that amount of money, what answers will I find? What really lies underneath there… Why am I tying my worth and value to money?

The layers of allowing are dense and rife. And each and every day you might find new parts of yourself that still feel like they are being allowed, but the journey to finding ourselves is a journey of creating freedom within. It is a journey of being sovereign and owning that. No-one has to allow me to do anything in this life. The only one here allowing anything is me, the human, the one who is ultimately in control. Not even your Soul is in control, she is your guidance system. She is the beautiful part of you that steers from a place of true unconditional love.

MY RESPONSIBILITY

If you think of your journey as an onion with many different layers. If you peel onions they make you cry but they are a delicious part of your meal, so you go through the pain for the pleasure. So, think about the fact that pulling back different layers of yourself will often be hard and even make you cry but the reward outweighs the few tears shed along the way. I always see the Divine Soul sitting right in the center of the onion, and the more I peel the closer I get to hearing her. The more layers there are the more muffled her voice is but the deeper I dig, the better I hear her guidance.

Bypassing the process of peeling away the layers is always an option, but do you really want to do that? Taking responsibility for your process with joy and excitement makes it so much easier.

> When you read the parts of this section, did any of it ring true for you?
>
> Where are you still bypassing?
>
> Awareness is always key…

LIGHT LANGUAGE

In 2016, I was with my Soul Sister friend for a healing session and as she was busy working on my energy body, she suddenly asked if I knew what Light Language was. It felt important and right there and then we both jumped on our phones and started Googling. As I started looking, I found a line speaking about Andromedan Light Language and I stopped. The article spoke about speaking in tongues and my heart skipped a beat.

When I was 16 years old, I was baptised in church. And then after that I started speaking a few strange words. At that stage we were in the Apostolic church as a family and people speaking in tongues were a regular occurrence and nothing weird or strange. So it was only natural after I was baptised that this would happen as the belief was that the Holy Spirit would speak through you. I connected with these words, but it made me feel uncomfortable, so I just left it. I mean what do you really know at 16, right? It was weird gobbledygook, and I didn't get it.

But now this concept came up again, 20 years later and I was curious. It was like instant recall remembering the few words that were on repeat in my head way back then. I started investigating and found some amazing books and watched loads of videos to understand more.

Light Language is a transmission of energy. As I have mentioned before everything is energy. Our bodies and spiritual beings are connected to this energy. Each of us can translate this energy. We do this through speaking Light Language, singing it, signing or drawing it.

And when you allow this energy to come through you as the channel it goes out into the world and hits the energy field of those who hear, see, or feel it. Once this energy (light codes) hits the energy body of another it changes certain aspects for them. It can facilitate deep healing. It can open parts of them that are waiting to be unlocked. It connects them to a deep remembering of who they are. It also helps to reconnect them with the state of oneness and love.

Each and every one of us are channels for different energies. And these energies that we transmit help others to heal and grow and it also helps Mother Gaia.

Initially, I was so scared of the weirdness of it all. I went on my very first retreat the day after I got married to my now husband in 2016. Yes, I know it sounds weird, but it just worked out that way and he was super sweet about me spending 10 days away in nature, sleeping outside in the wild and swimming with dolphins. It is still a big joke that I went on my honeymoon with a bunch of complete strangers.

But on this beautiful retreat in nature, I allowed myself to fully reconnect with my Light Language. During one of our healing sessions, I felt the deep need to speak this unknown language, but it scared me so much that I got up and left the circle. Our facilitator knew what was happening and she took me aside and gave me a good talking to. She made me see how keeping this hidden would not be serving anyone and that the time was right now for me to fully connect with this ability.

I spent the next week on retreat chanting Light Language to the Earth, the Sky and the Sea. I kept on repeating what was coming up in my head and it just felt like more and more wanted to come up, so I just allowed it. I did not know what to do with it, but I trusted that in time I would understand more.

When I got back home, I spoke to my circle of Soul Sisters and during one of our weekly meetings, I asked if I could share what had happened and the new language with them. It was so good to be in a circle of people that I could trust and to share what was happening. They were amazingly supportive and encouraged me to keep on channelling. Then a few weeks later I was invited to do a Light Language session for another healing circle that I was part of. I was so nervous and totally petrified but something inside me kept pushing me to do this. It was an amazing first group session, I channelled different languages for each person there and it just started flowing.

I knew it was super weird and freaky, but the love that people felt, and the shifts and healing was profound, and I just had to let go of the judgment and keep doing what I was doing. It was helping people and healing people and after all that was what my Soul wanted to do.

Initially, I did not understand what all the different words meant or the signs that my hands started making but I also realised that my ego did not have to be involved in the process. My human need to understand everything and make sense of everything did not apply to this work.

All that mattered was that I knew I was connecting with energy that was for the highest good of myself and those that I worked with. And whatever the person that heard my words needed would be taken care of by their Higher Self. Their energy system and Soul knew exactly what they needed in that moment and would work with it as needed.

There are many different energies that we can connect with and it all depends on your intention and what you are working with. As you do this work longer and start to delve deeper you will be able to specifically call on the energies you want to work with. Light Language connects us to various energies – it can be Galactic, Angelic, Earth or Elemental.

Speaking is the most common and well-known way of connecting with Light Language. Singing of the languages and making different sounds is another way that you can start connecting with the language.

You must look at the process of channelling Light Language as being a vessel for light transmissions. You are connecting with an energy out there and then bringing that energy forth into the world through your voice. The codes and healing energies move through your being out of your voice box and into the environment around you and hit the light body of the people hearing your voice travelling across space and time.

The less attached you are to the outcome of your channelling the easier it becomes. The longer I worked with the energies, the more I got a feeling / sense / message connected to the energies – I like to call it a theme. I would know that the energy is for heart healing or for manifestation or for empowerment. Only now after 5 years of doing this work, can I translate certain aspects fully and use the language to communicate back to the energies that I am working with. Again, it all takes practice like riding a bike.

Another way of connecting with the energy is through signing. Just like with Reiki energy, you can move the energy that you are channelling through your hands into the world. Once you connect to the energy, you allow your hands to start moving as they need to. When I do a transmission, my hands are often going crazy, and it always feels to me like I am literally moving energy around into specific forms and patterns that then is also transmitted to the receivers. For me this comes automatically when I speak the language, but for other's they literally just move their hands and will not do any talking.

Drawing is another way of channelling the light codes for people to receive. These are high vibrational signatures and shapes that carry codes within them. And when you connect with the art/drawing/writing it activates and/or heals something within you. There are even tattoo artists channelling light codes and putting it on their client's bodies. The possibilities are endless, so do yourself a favour and go and see what is out there. Light Language art is quite spectacular.

I keep seeing visions of how all these little light towers are standing on the Earth and receiving light beams into them and then spreading that out over the surface of the Earth. We are constantly receiving light codes and healing codes from the Cosmos and we can share this with other people out there. I also feel like the words that we speak are keys to unlocking the consciousness of humanity even further.

So, if you are feeling a language within you, please pay attention. Your words and art are needed by the world. It helps people to reconnect back to their own Divinity again. And in turn we are giving light to Mother Gaia, but we are also receiving light codes from her to share with the world.

Oh, and as an aside, for me and many of my clients, the shower is a great place to start practicing. We are in water firstly, which is clearing our energies, and secondly there is no-one there to judge you whilst you start speaking your weird language. So take some time and give it a try. One word or sentence at a time…

Repeat, repeat, repeat. It will eventually come streaming out, I promise.

DNA ACTIVATION

And so, after a gypsy card reading by one of my closest Soul Sisters in August 2018, I went home and told the husband that we needed to move back to England. He is British and had been thinking about it for quite a while. But me being South African and having lived in London for a year when we first met I just could not imagine myself back in the UK again. But the message in the reading that day was so obvious and strong and I knew that I needed to follow my gut and just jump. As I always say, never ask if you are not going to listen to the answer.

He was ready and it all dovetailed perfectly with his business and him also needing to be back in England to support a big company transition. We chose to move to East Devon. We eventually moved from South Africa at the end of June 2019 and settled in the most gorgeous part of England. Everything worked out beautifully for all three of us.

A dear friend then told me about her Radical Guide DNA Activation™ with The Woo Collective™ and something inside me jumped. I needed to check it out and see what it was all about. As I started reading more about their work and seeing references to some concepts that I had been wanting to learn more about. I knew this was something I needed to do. The work was linked to Mary Magdalene and I had started working with her energy at the end of 2018 and learning more about her, but I was not sure why she showed up.

What is Radical Guide DNA Activation™?

Your spiritual and cosmic DNA strands are connected to your Soul. These beautiful strands that we all have are the life force of your energy body but they are dormant. This Quantum Healing modality was channelled from Mary Magdalene to restore and activate your dormant spiritual strands of DNA. During the process of activating DNA, your strands are repaired and re-activated. This is done through clearing stagnant dense energy from Past Lives, removing various Seals from your energy body and showing you dormant information coded into your strands that is specifically relevant to you. The process of showing you who you are helps you to step back into your power and purpose. This work helps you to hear your Soul again and work with her in a much deeper and more aligned way than ever before.

In August 2019, I had my first 24 strands activated and things started shifting for me. Then in September as I was in France on a Mary Magdalene retreat, I had the next 24 strands activated there. It was an amazing retreat and a huge shift in my connection with her and my consciousness.

She opened up my consciousness to the Sacred Marriage between the Divine Feminine and the Divine Masculine. She showed me how I was on a journey of healing the Divine Feminine within me and how my journey through the patriarchy of many lifetimes brought me back to myself. On the retreat we visited a forest where I saw myself being assaulted by a group of men in a previous life. It was one of the scariest experiences I had ever had but I knew that I had to confront that pain there and then. And again, it reminded me of the wounding that we carry within us through the lifetimes that we have been in existence. It also confirmed for me that these hurt parts within us need to be seen and dealt with even if they are not from this present life. So never diminish the impact that your Past Lives have on your current life. So many of our fears, insecurities and shadows are linked to what happened there.

The DNA Activation lead me back to the archetype of the High Priestess. She had started showing up for me when I visited Peru in 2018. Whilst spending the day with the Shaman in the ruins we had a ceremony in a part of the ruins that was a sacred space for the priestesses of those times. As I connected with the energy of the ground there, I saw this beautiful woman standing in front of me. She was powerful and rather intimidating, but she made herself known to me. She told me that she was rising again and that I could choose to work with her again now.

So, I allowed her to merge with my energy and took her back home with me. At the time I did not understand what it meant or why she showed herself to me, but I knew it would become clear to me at a later stage. When I found out after my DNA Activation that this archetype had shown up in my report I knew that it was time. I knew that I had to start embodying the attributes of the High Priestess in my work and in my life.

The process of the Seal Removal in my DNA Activations shifted so much for me. These Seals that have been placed on our energy bodies stop us from fully connecting to the flow of energy within ourselves, but it also diminishes our ability to connect with the energies outside of us. I always say it felt like the blinkers were taken off my eyes. My world opened up after my activations and my consciousness started expanding in ways that I am still not even able to put into words.

During the years of reading the Akashic Records I developed my Claircognizance (clear knowing). It was my most prominent Clair-ability and I always laugh as my Clairvoyant friend always reminded me how I chose the most difficult of the Clairs to work with. I didn't really know any better at that point in time when I started so I just had to trust that the knowing was right. So then when I did the DNA Activation part of the work to connect me deeper to my primary Clair-ability, what came up for me was quite surprising and I was a little shocked, to say the least. I was told that my guides wanted me to start connecting with my Clairvoyant abilities. And I was slightly annoyed by all this to be honest!

I had woken up a few times in my life with strange beings and people that have passed over next to my bed and my heart literally felt like it had stopped. There is nothing worse than waking up with a stranger next to your bed especially living in a country like South Africa where house robberies at night are quite a common occurrence. I remember early on asking my guides to please stop showing up like this. Surely there was a better way to connect and talk? So I stuck to my Claircognizance. I also had no desire to walk through life having to look at dead people and spirits everywhere, it just freaked me out.

In my report it became clear that I needed to start working on this ability again. So I struck a bit of a deal with my guides. I would be very happy to see whatever I needed to see but with my eyes closed. I started practising this and it has been absolutely wonderful. They happily showed me all that I need to see for myself and for my clients whilst I sit with my eyes closed. I now have my own private movie playing behind my eyelids. And this was where my channelling abilities started taking off.

After my own activations I signed up to become a Radical Guide DNA Activation™ practitioner and activate DNA for others. I knew I had to work with the energy of Mary Magdalene and that there were some new and exciting adventures waiting for me. Learning from the beautiful Soul owners of The Woo Collective™ taught me so much about accepting my darkness, my shadows and being real in my pursuit of authentic spirituality. These women helped me to see through a lot of the bullshit whitewashed spirituality that flows through the world at this point in time.

I also realised how important the DNA Activations were in the process of opening me up to receive information from my Soul and from the energies outside of me. I was more determined than ever to start activating others so they could also experience this magic and connect with their deepest gifts again. This work gave me the opportunity to remember my ability to channel and bring information forth for others. The DNA Activations helped me to find my true Soul voice again and work through the fear of sharing this voice. It was liberating and freeing. And I wanted everyone else to feel this too.

As I returned from my retreat something inside me was stirring to create. I kept returning to a vision of sacred geometry – a circle with a dot in the middle…

And then the pieces started to drop in. I had a conversation with a Soul Sister about the medicine wheels used by certain Native American groups and then I started seeing how things were falling into place. I did some research and found information about the Andromedans being involved in bringing the stone circles to Earth and I knew I found my connection. The Star Beings have been sharing information with us through the circles for thousands of years. I just needed to go back and find out what I needed to remember.

I also remembered a process that I was shown when I visited a sacred stone circle in South Africa and I knew that there was a link there.

And so I started channelling the Starseed Sacred Circle and created a process for getting back to the essence of your being, finding your own Soul voice again and trusting yourself.

I worked with the energies of Mother Gaia, the Andromedans, Sirius, Pleiades and the Arcturians.

All of these energies wanted to be part of the process of finding and knowing the Self again. I slowly started putting it all together and the Sacred Circle was born. The Circle was the inspiration behind this book and lead me back to deep parts of myself and my truth.

THE PATRIARCHY

I was never really aware of my issues with the patriarchy until I moved to the UK. Now to say that the patriarchy did not present in my life in many shapes and forms before would be wrong. It was there since childhood. I just never took the time to understand what I was feeling and how deeply I carried those wounds within me.

I grew up in a lineage of very strong women, my Mom's mom, my Granny who passed when I was two, was the ultimate rebel. Driving around wearing trousers and making her own money in a time when women were supposed to be in the kitchen cooking, was really frowned upon. But the stories I hear about her and how amazing she was and also really into woo woo, makes my heart sing. I also love that she is always first in the queue whenever mediums tap into my energy, excited to talk to me and shouting instructions loudly from beyond on how I should be doing things.

So she raised a daughter, my Mom, who also turned into a strong woman, someone who from a young age was extremely self-aware and wise. My Mom really cheered me on to independence and free thinking and turned a blind eye to the hippie daughter running around in high school with bare feet, weird clothes and ideas. She has always been a great supporter of my work and ideas and has never asked me to not be me. Although I am sure she sometimes wonders where I really come from. My Dad and her are still happily married and I love the fact that she can be herself and stand up for her beliefs in their relationship. It's a fiery one, but it taught me that I did not need to back down when a man challenged my ideas or plans in life.

This upbringing made for interesting times when it came to my work life. I always remember when I took my first high ranking job at a bank back in South Africa, and my Dad warning me that I need to be careful as it could suck my Soul dry. He had spent most of his adult life working in the banking industry and knew what he was talking about. But me all young and feisty joined a powerful female team in the bank and created a kick ass squad.

The only thing was that we all had to behave like the men to be seen and heard – our masculine energies ruling the team and leaving little space for our true creative expressions and feminine energies to show up. It was a tough learning school and when my female boss left and a male boss took over my world really started turning upside down. Constantly watching him take credit for my hard work and hours of dedication to my craft just wore me down. And every time I dared to shed a tear about how unhappy or disempowered I felt, it just again enforced the belief that girls don't belong here. You are too soft and full of emotions to cut it in this man's world.

But I pushed ahead, left that company and joined one of the biggest firms in South Africa in the banking industry. I showed up even more in my extreme masculine energy and ran circles around my male colleagues – boldly insisting on crazy increases and bonuses to make myself feel worthier and then pulling it off as well. In hindsight, I now understand that the only way I could measure my worth was through money and my corporate job title. This is a massive part of my journey that I am still unlearning today.

Through my various roles in corporate, I kept on supressing my feminine side, always having to work so much harder than all the men just to prove that I belonged. This took a massive toll on me and I am still learning how to not swallow down my unhappiness with unjust situations. I am still learning how to stand up for myself and how to be in my masculine and feminine power together.

The structures of the patriarchy run very deep within us all. And part of my journey here on earth is to unravel the patriarchy in myself.

There I said it.

As much as I had feelings of anger, resentment and rage against the systems that oppress so many of us I had to go through a huge journey of deep understanding and this lead me back to a profound epiphany.

I was visiting a Dolmen site with a dear Soul Sister in 2020. Dolmens are believed to be ancient burial sites, consisting of two or more upright slabs, often weighing hundreds of pounds with a roof slab placed on top. This was usually covered with stones and sands to form a tomb of sorts. Through years of erosion we are left with the skeleton of the structure of which you can see across various sites in Europe and Africa.

And in my usual Yolandi fashion I didn't really understand this deep and intense need to visit this site and what I would find there, all I knew was it was calling very loudly and I needed to go.

As we started working with the energies of the site there was so much that was shown to me. I saw myself as a young priestess being thrown out of the group for speaking the truth about the injustice of what was happening at that time. At the same time I also saw myself as the one inflicting the injustice on the group. It was hard to watch all of this unfolding at this site and the Past Life hurts presenting themselves to me so clearly. I spent time releasing and forgiving those parts of myself there but I did not yet see the bigger picture.

I was so busy focusing on what the patriarchy had done and the wounds inflicted by the patriarchy on everyone out there. I was constantly being in that space of placing it all outside of me, all the anger and the feelings and what was happening in the world.

Then eventually, out of the blue one day, it struck me. I was carrying the patriarchy within myself. I had taken on the conditioning and the structures and the way of being of the patriarchy within myself...

MY TAKE

Our journey as humanity with the patriarchy goes back a very, very long time. And please note that I am not a historian, scholar or expert, so again this is my interpretation and truth around the concept. Also note that I was brought up in a Christian household, so part of my journey here is to look at my ancestral lineage and understand it on a deeper level.

Back in ancient times we were all revering the Great Mother. Modern day archaeologists have found beautiful relics and statues of the Great Mother dating back as far as 35,0000 years ago. The ancients believed that she was in charge, all came from her and through her. We were all very deeply connected to her. And so life was lived connected to Mother Nature, following our hearts, inclusivity and community. The whole mission was to live together, to survive and thrive. And then as time moved on and humans started feeling into power and greed, the need to own more and wield more power became a driving force.

Whenever I feel into the time before the masculine became unbalanced, I always feel like there was this mutual respect between the male and female energies. Within ourselves we managed to be in balance. We hold both these energies within us and keeping them in balance makes for a beautiful life, but when we start leaning too much into one or the other, things start to go a bit haywire. We become too dominant or too submissive, too controlling or too fearful.

And eventually we ended up thousands of years ago in a world that moved from balance into a world that embraced hierarchy, power and greed. And humanity started to change. Our beautiful Divine Blueprints started to alter their natural state to fit into the new mould that was introduced to the world around us. We needed to fit in to survive. The slow erosion of the understanding of our connection to Mother Earth and each other started. We gradually started forgetting more and more.

But lucky for us there were many groups of amazing humans who were still on a mission to bring back equality and connection to all that is. These incredible Souls fought hard to keep the ancient ways alive. Often they had to keep things secret and hidden in order for it to be preserved, but they kept teaching and sharing and reminding all those around them of the presence of a Divine connection that we all had within us right from the start.

And this brings me to the story of Master Jesus and Mary Magdalene. They were the representation of the Divine Masculine and Divine Feminine energies coming together. An introduction to the new energies of the Christ Consciousness and a revolution within.

Working together in their lifetime to educate and undo old ways of thinking, old ways of pushing down the Divine Feminine and creating balance. Now I know that for many of us the history reflects Mary Magdalene as a whore who had seven demons driven out of her by Master Jesus. Recent discoveries show that she had her own set of scriptures like the male apostles and that Master Jesus and her where much closer than any of us were taught in the Bible.

And my take on this little diversion in history is that around 400CE a bunch of old nervous men got together in a room, and started talking about this new religion called Christianity. They were a tad stressed out by it as this concept of being able to connect directly to the Divine and being in control of your own life and destiny would give the people under their rule way too much freedom. The societal structure at that time was very much governed by hierarchical rule – the Emperor on top, everyone else below and women were basically just above slaves right at the bottom of the ladder. But these new Christian thinkers were talking about equality and how we were all connected and the same. The teachings of Master Jesus and Mary Magdalene were starting to spread and become more accepted by the masses.

There were of course the Pagan religions that were very big at that time too and so they would have to create a new system that took some of those Pagan ideas and weaved it into the Christian ideas of the time, but sprinkle in some hierarchy and fear and they would have a pretty awesome little recipe book for controlling the masses. Surely there needed to be some kind of bad guy in the mix and if you stepped out of line a bit of burning in the flames of hell would keep them under control?

So they started taking out bits and pieces from the scriptures, ancient myths and legends that they knew and copied and pasted these together. In the process making sure that women remained at the bottom of the ladder and that sexuality was controlled and made to be something rather evil and dirty. Because they believed that women had been using that little gift for centuries to control and manipulate mankind.

Lucky for us modern humans, some super clever monks decided to bury scrolls in various places in the desert (Dead Sea Scrolls and Nag Hammadi in case you want to go and read a bit more about the history) and this then enabled us, in this modern day to find, translate and piece together some parts of history that the dudes in Rome did not deem necessary to include in their life manifesto named the Bible. A book that has controlled the lives of a huge number of humans for almost 2,000 years.

It was a strategy based on creating fear and separation. Removing the beautiful concept that Pagan and Christian teachings held at that time that we were connected to all. From that point forward the reign of terror started in that part of the world and branched out across the planet. Priests were running around telling everyone that would listen that they needed to come through them to get to the Divine. And the best part is obviously that we were all born sinners. So you literally didn't have a snowballs chance in hell of ever getting into heaven unless you obeyed the 10 commandments and paid your taxes to the Emperor. And any other form of Pagan worshipping of anything other than 'God' would also send you straight to hell. So all of a sudden everyone was doomed!

I sometimes sit and wonder what it would have been like in those years. Here you were happily dancing around in circles honouring the Great Mother and some guy waltzes in and tells you, stop now or burn in the eternal fires of hell. Or maybe you were an all zen Christian guy connecting with the Divine and loving everyone else and another guy in some purple fancy robe walks up to you and tells you nope, sorry buddy, you have to come and listen to me now, no more knowing that you can just go directly to the big guy, you have to come through me now, I am the new gatekeeper to the Divine.

It must have been one huge mission to get so many people to start listening. So many executions, torturing, suffering and lies to get people so scared and full of fear to turn them away from what made their hearts happy and kept them free.

When I feel into that time, my heart is so filled with pain, my insides literally hurt and I can't even begin to imagine what the next 1,000 years were like for those who wanted to stay free. Those who just wanted to be in that space of loving each other and living their lives close to the Divine.

And so many of our wounds as lightworkers are connected to those times. We were forced to disconnect from our truths, not speak up or dying to try and speak our truths. It was an intense time in history.

THE PERSECUTED

So when I started working with this patriarchy concept I was filled with rage. The more I discovered and read about the manipulation and pain caused, the angrier I got. My insides were on fire for the injustice and the pain inflicted on humanity.

I saw many lifetimes of being persecuted for my beliefs and my longing for the truth and for freedom.

I saw so many humans in that space of pain and fear. Constantly trying to stand up for their beliefs, fighting hard but also fearing for their lives, their loved ones and just trying to survive.

And all of this for money, land and power?

Talk about feeling a bit jaded and enraged, right? So here as humanity we stood before two choices – give our power away or take it back. Such a big part of our learning journey here on this planet is to learn to take our power back, set our boundaries and become sovereign and free again.

For such a long time I lived with a fear deep inside me. I was truly fearful of my own power and of the misuse of power too. Not other's misusing it but me taking my power and forcing it upon others, and to be very honest, this is an ongoing struggle in my unravelling process that is constantly being shown to me. Am I forcing my power on others, am I honouring their journeys and not trying to manipulate and bully them into my way of seeing the world?

My very first encounter with my own power struggle was in Egypt. I was on a beautiful retreat with some amazing Goddesses and part of my reason for going was to step up. At that stage, I had been working with the Akashic Records for about two years but I was feeling stuck and realised that my Soul wanted to speak up more, be heard more in different ways, but I was petrified. Something inside me was holding me back. Before the trip, I had become aware of a Past Life where I literally lead loads of people to their death because of my bad judgement and choices, and all I could think about was the fact that I might be doing the same thing again in this lifetime. What if I was responsible again for such atrocities?

And when I got to Egypt, during our opening ceremony I had this huge lion face right in front of me during meditation. I did not understand it, but as usual I knew I just needed to let things unfold. And then the next morning, as we walked into the first temple next to the Nile I saw lions everywhere, and here was my first introduction to the amazing Goddess called Sekhmet. The lion-headed Goddess of war and healing.

A few days later we had the privilege of visiting a very small and ancient temple with a life-size statue of her, still perfectly preserved more than 3,000 years on. This little temple was hidden away in the great Karnak complex. It was one of my most profound spiritual experiences. The guard who was looking after the little temple came through and started doing amazing healing rituals on us as we were sat in front of this statue. I had a beautiful experience of release there and as I then moved to one of the other little rooms all by myself I had a vision of her asking me to step forward. To take that one step to committing to my Soul. I still remember myself physically taking a step forward and as I did that the sunlight from a very small window hit my face in this dark room. It was such a symbolic moment of enlightenment for me. It was the start. I had made a promise to myself in that moment that I would keep walking towards the light again, no matter how scary it was. There was and still is, a lot of healing for me to do around power, but I have learnt that we all carry it deep within. It is our sovereign right to be in our power, to take it back and to use it wisely.

One thing this experience taught me was that we all have choices. We can choose to be the victim of abuse of power or we can choose change.

The injustices of thousands of years are deeply ingrained in all of us.

THE PERSECUTOR

BUT as much as we have been persecuted and we carry our Starseed Wounds and our Witch Wounds and all our other wounds from centuries of fighting for the light, there is another side to this story.

'Every coin has two sides', my guides said to me with a little giggle. I was not amused as I had just had a massive realisation that literally made my insides turn.

I woke up one morning and my friend told me that one of her friends had dreamt about me the night before. And I just started crying. I struggled to breathe and was starting to hyperventilate and could not understand what was happening. I didn't even know this person but something felt very, very wrong. She had told me about a lifetime of her friend being in Italy during the witch hunts. I knew I was there, but something felt wrong. I calmed myself down and later in the day I took some time to sit with this weird outburst of emotions. And as I started walking back in time on my own timeline I saw myself there giving the orders to kill the witches. It was me, I was the one persecuting them…

I met her that afternoon on a Zoom call and it is always lovely to introduce yourself for the very first time and then promptly apologise for killing someone in a Past Life. Well, that is how it went down, but she sent me the most remarkable message that evening, that put so many things into perspective for me.

'I've always believed that we each have a team of souls that are like family. Before we incarnate on earth, they sit around a table and decide who will play which part in that person's life and who will teach each lesson. I was always told that the people who treat us the worst are the souls that love us the most because they chose the most difficult lessons to teach us, so if you did, in one life, play a part in executing me as a witch, I honestly believe that your soul did it from a place of love because you chose to be that defining character in that lifetime of mine.'

Reading this message made my heart stop. I have always had visions of us Souls sitting around tables discussing the lifetime ahead and seeing how we can help each other. But her words about how much we love each other, really hit me hard. And it made me realise that all those lives where I also did wrong and hurt others, it was a Soul choice from a place of deep love.

So if you hold any ideas or fears about having harmed or done things wrong in a Past Life, I can guarantee that you have, but it is part of polarity. Dark and light. You have to experience all of it to learn and grow and understand all the aspects of your being. So trying to hold onto it and use it as an excuse not to take back your power again is doing yourself a disservice.

Every coin has two sides – dark and light – I am here to experience it all!

This incident then made me look deeply at my judgement of 'bad' people. Now, I am not saying that it is okay to go around hurting other humans. No! But I need to start seeing where people are coming from. The old saying is 'hurt people, hurt people'. These humans have signed up for a life where they choose an intense path of learning. We all have free will, right? In that lifetime where I chose to harm her, I could have chosen differently.

I could have chosen to heal my own wounds and not inflict them on someone else, but I didn't and that is also part of what I have to learn. I make unconscious decisions all the time, but to keep judging myself about them, just won't do. It was a mistake that I am learning from still and I can choose to be scared that I will do it again OR I can learn to trust myself.

I am learning to trust that I will stay in conscious awareness of all my choices.

Every day, as I make choices on how to show up in the world for myself, for my family, for my friends, clients and humans I don't know, I make a choice. I choose to underpin all my choices with love.

Now don't get me wrong, there are a LOAD of times where I don't do this, we all do right? Sometimes I am driven by fear, guilt, shame or obligation. But I see this and I know this. And then off I go to unravel where these underlying feelings come from and next time I don't do it again. I try harder to do better. Every single day.

It is just a process. All of our lives are about learning to show up in a space of love more often. And you won't get it right all the time, you would not be human if you did. I would be asking you to go and join some epic monks in a cave in Tibet somewhere if you did. This is 3D life, this is hard and things are complicated and tough some days.

Our awareness brings us closer to love each day. So just keep showing up and living and forgiving yourself, it is all we can do.

MY CHOICE

So after the whole me murdering other humans incident (here is me laughing at myself), I had to face the facts.

I could stay in that patriarchal energy of judgement and be cross and angry with 'them' for doing this and for life being in such a state of patriarchy or I could start doing something.

My personal ancestral lineage is littered with judgement, oppression and power hungry games. I am after all a white Afrikaans South African. You can't get a more messed up lineage than that, right? Apartheid was the brainchild of my ancestors after all.

It took me a long time to work through that and get my ideas and my feelings into perspective, and I am still having to look at it each day.

I also realised that my lineage made me scared of stepping out of line. We were taught from a young age that you have to conform and do as the powers that be say or you will be punished. Like the millions of non-white people in South Africa

Just like the church used to say to the masses, 'If you don't listen and conform, you will burn in hell for eternity'.

But there comes a point in each of our lives when we have to make a choice to stop conforming to the belief of separateness. I have to make a choice to come from a place where I start seeing everyone as equal, where I realise that we are all humans with great big hearts and beautiful Souls. Each and every one of us. There is no exception.

So I am choosing to not oppress others with my beliefs, my truths and my ideas. I am choosing to share these freely. We are entitled to our truths and our beliefs; my only request is that you think about their roots.

If our truths and our beliefs are rooted in love and compassion – what would change?

How would you change?

How would you show up in the world?

SOUL-LED REVOLUTION

Our work as conscious beings now is to start introducing balance. The unbalanced masculine energy has affected ALL humans. Some humans have benefited greatly from this distorted way and others have suffered greatly. So this is not a fight between masculine and feminine energies. Because again both sides of the coin story here – the feminine has also oppressed and harmed in many ways. She hasn't always been innocent in history/herstory.

My work within myself is to get both my masculine and feminine energies in balance. Go into both parts of myself and see where my wounds lie. As there are wounds in both parts. And when I heal those I bring more balance. And eventually I am able to get back into that space of what is called the sacred union or marriage. Where these two parts of myself love and respect each other and they create a union within me that is wrapped in love and compassion.

And when I show up in the world from that sacred union space, things around me will start changing.

The fighting within me, the striving that I carry within my own being is directly reflected in the world around me. The world is a giant mirror for how we all battle within ourselves each day.

The more I deal with my war inside of myself, the world will respond. The war inside me is fuelled by judgement.

We fear judgement from those around us, to the point of completely stopping ourselves from showing up in the world. We wake up each day wanting to be more of who we are, but then the judgement record starts playing again. How will everyone outside perceive me and my words and my ideas? We stop shining, we stop being our most authentic selves because we fear judgement more than anything else in this world.

So why do we fear this? In our deepest memories going back all the way to the beginning of time, if you were different or did not fit into the mould the tribe would kick you out. You would have to leave the cave, the food supplies and the security of the shelter that you had. You would be all alone, vulnerable and you might get eaten by a bear or a lion or starve to death. Either way being different equals death.

But now life is slightly different, you probably have a job and a house and are pretty awesome at looking after yourself right? So what is the worst that can happen? Well, you might get kicked out of your family and rejected by friends and loved ones, but you won't die. And again, I love the ego because that is where it always goes first, the worst case scenario. But what if everyone lovingly accepted your uniqueness? What if they just shrugged their shoulders and went, 'Okay, so she is being a bit weird but it is fine'.

I know for me coming out of the spiritual weird-ass closet was a big thing. Coming from a Christian upbringing to all of a sudden turn around and say – Well, I now believe in reincarnation, Starseeds and being able to speak to guides and angels…

I thought my family was going to burn me at the stake. But they didn't. My Mom was intrigued and asked for a reading and my Dad listened and said it's all fine but he won't be changing his beliefs. So we all agreed to disagree but still love each other. And no-one was burnt at the stake or abandoned or rejected. We are still on great terms as I descend further and further into my spiritual weirdness.

Of course, I lost very close friends and there were instances where it hurt when people threw judgement my way, but I survived and found new friends that accepted me and loved my weirdness and ideas. The husband, having been an observer of this entire journey, still doesn't understand half of what I do or how I live, but he knows the person that I am. He knows my heart and he loves me for that. He has been one of my greatest teachers and supporters over the years.

Fearing the judgement of others is linked to the judgement of self. Understanding my judgements is such a big part of the journey to finding myself and my true essence. Looking at where I don't feel worthy or loved is a great eye-opener. Understanding where I am rejecting and abandoning parts of myself shows me why I fear those things from people around me.

Judgement creates a war. War brings destruction, sadness and loss.

So what stops a war? Revolution stops a war…

But traditionally we would take one truth and then push another perceived truth onto it by force. Now is not the time for this. Now is the time to stop the war within you.

Starting this revolution begins with me. Wanting the world to change begins with me. The more I am in denial of who I really am, the more I fuel the war.

Getting back to my true Soul essence is an act of revolution. My commitment to finding myself again and unravelling my own patriarchal structures within will change the world. And the best part is that I can do it however I choose; the only requirement is to be true to who I am. This can be done in a million different ways, there is no right or wrong.

And the moment I start the work, those around me feel it, they will start seeing me in a different light. Me allowing myself to move back to who I am inspires others, but it will also frighten some. And that is okay.

The patriarchal systems within us are rooted in fear. So there will be those who are scared of us changing. They might want to stop us or judge us. But it is our job to just keep going. It is also my responsibility to recognise that their truth is different to mine, and that is okay.

When I step into the space of seeing, hearing and feeling all of what someone is, and I can recognise my wounds in them as well, I am making a start. The world has a very big divide at the moment. And sometimes it feels insurmountable. But what helps me is to understand that we all come from a different place, we all wear those sunglasses of our own truth. My truth and your truth are underpinned with our pain and wounds. And if we can step into acceptance and into the space of Divine empathy for each other, then we are making a huge difference already. When we stop killing and hurting each other because we believe different things, the world will start changing.

And in those moments when you can't understand someone's point of view or truth, educate yourself. Take a moment to see where they are coming from.

I know for me I have some truths that are non-negotiable and that I refuse to change for anyone, for example abuse of others. And I will be firm in my truth around these issues, but I can't make someone else change their mind. What I can do is speak out about issues, I can educate myself about issues and I can show up in the world supporting those causes. I can make my voice heard without breaking others down. I can make my voice count by speaking from my Soul and not my wounds.

And when I encounter someone that does not hold these truths, I do take a moment to think about where they come from, how they were raised and wounded. I take a moment to acknowledge and accept that this is their reality and their truth. But it doesn't mean I am going to change my truth, and it also does not mean that I become judge and jury of their truth. This is their journey, they will walk it and my job is to be firm in my own truth.

But you have to do the work. Your life will start changing the moment you allow yourself to not be held captive by the patriarchal repression that you carry within you. And again this is about you and I each making a choice to change. This is about us leading from our Souls.

We are all busy unlearning our outdated behaviours. We are becoming beautiful Divine vessels of light and healing and compassion for everyone out there. And by you becoming that vessel you help others do the same. Then we are infecting each other with love, infecting each other with compassion, we are creating a pandemic of compassion and of love. Wouldn't that be awesome?

Imagine if we could all come to a place of Divine Love within us, what would the world look like then?

> When I am in my truth I open the door for my Soul to speak freely.
>
> When I do my inner work I open the door for my Soul to speak freely.
>
> When I connect with my heart portal I open the door for my Soul to speak freely.

Finding my truth again will lead me back to my Soul and my Soul will lead me back to Divine Love. The beginning and end of it all.

The Soul-led revolution can begin…

THE JOURNEY

THE STARSEED SACRED CIRCLE

The Circle was created as a download and a remembering of how to return to myself and my own inner wisdom. The picture below is a representation of the journey we will follow together to remember your Soul connection and your own inner knowing. Remembering who you truly are, your authentic self.

I always felt that we had forgotten how to listen to our Souls. Through my life journey and learnings I realised that I was always taking a similar path, following a spiral journey back to a place of knowing myself deeper and deeper. And when this download came to me it took all of what I had learnt, all the beautiful energies that I have connected with over the years and put it into a single process that I could help others walk through. A process that has helped many to find themselves again, to step out of judgement and ever closer to their Soul voice.

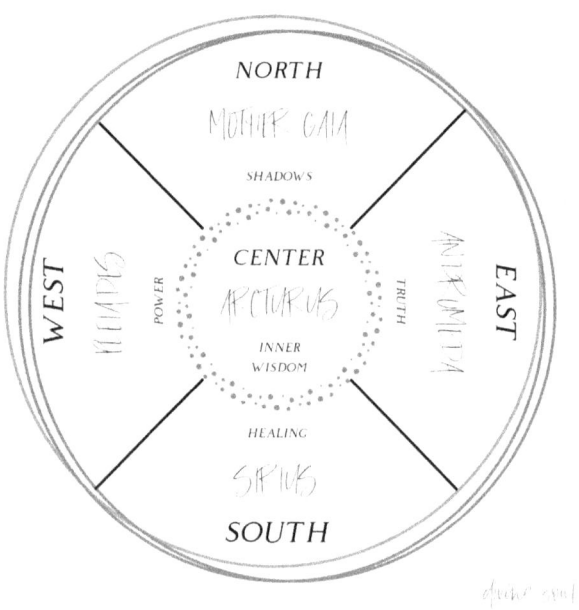

If possible, please make sure you have a journal handy whilst working through the Circle. It is really helpful to be able to look back at the work that you have completed and also to see how you have changed and grown.

The more I commit myself to my journey of self-discovery the more I can feel my Soul. I have a choice in life to blindly walk forward without ever stopping and questioning myself, my fears, my truths and ideas. But the magic starts when I allow myself to question everything. If I am brave enough to go and look in the darkness and try and understand myself, my Soul jumps up and down with excitement.

I know people often state that we have to reconnect to the Soul. I don't agree with that statement. I am walking a journey of remembering that she is actually right here. She never left, she never wanted to not be heard, seen or felt. She is patiently waiting for me to be ready to listen, see and feel her. She is a constant in my existence. But she is waiting for me to put my hand up and proclaim that I am ready to work with her. She is endlessly sending signs and helping those desires and feelings within me to rise. She is sending signs to help me remember.

What if you allowed yourself to commit to an eyes and ears wide open policy?

You are more ready than you think otherwise we wouldn't be sitting here together connecting via my book.

The Sacred Circle Journey takes us from North, to East, to South, to West and back to the Center. This journey is based on my experience of coming back to myself, the journey that I walked and the parts of me that I remembered over the years.

Every section focuses on a specific area of remembering. These areas are designed to help you to find yourself moving deeper towards who you are. Each area is also calling for you to be very honest with yourself. Sometimes we don't want to admit certain things about ourselves and those closest to us. The scary realisations lead us back to our Souls.

So prepare yourself to reconnect with your deep Soul desires, your truth, your flow, your power and your inner wisdom. Showing up with compassion is needed for this journey.

So allow me and my Soul to take your hand and show you more of you.

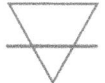

THE NORTH

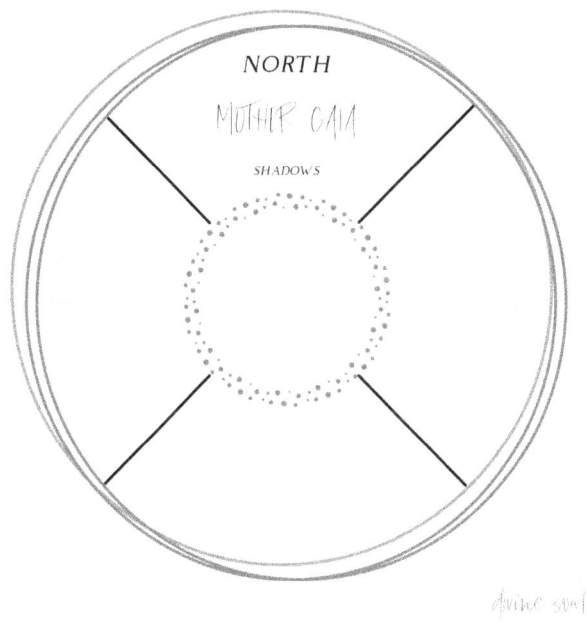

The first direction that we focus on is the North, your starting point for working with the Starseed Sacred Circle. The top of the Circle and the most grounded part of the Circle as it is linked to the energy of Earth. You will see that I refer to her as Mother Gaia in my writing. It is a term of respect and endearment.

Working in the North you will take the time to go deeper, to start the process of understanding your shadow and darkness. To get to the point of acceptance of your perceived darkness and discomfort, the place that you don't want to go. The things that scare us – that is where the magic lies. Our magic lies in our authentic self-expression.

Our Souls are calling us to be who we are, courageous in our pursuit of our own authenticity. And it takes a lot of courage to be real, to be you. But I know that is why you are here reading this. It is time to commit and start the process of being real.

This work allows you to look at the parts of you that you don't like or are hiding away from. Part of your process will be to engage with this shadow and work with it – to see it, to feel it and to consciously acknowledge it. This will result in clarity that will guide your way to the East.

We are creating inner vision for you and the ability to work with feelings and getting to know them and to accept them as part of the whole of your conscious being. Imagine this process as a merger of the conscious and the unconscious within you. This requires commitment and courage.

Our first step will be to reconnect with the deep desire hidden within your being. And this desire is what you will take through the Circle with you. When you recognise, accept, connect and heal around this, you start the process of reconnecting with who you are. BUT let's first start by explaining what we work with in this part of the Circle.

MOTHER GAIA

The energy of Mother Gaia is grounded and solid. Unwavering and totally rooted. Working with the energy of Earth, gives us the ability to go into the deeper parts of ourselves. To tap into the deep darkness within.

If you imagine the unknown of Mother Earth below the surface, there is so much no-one has ever seen. The concept is to allow yourself to become like Earth and excavate and explore deep within. Think of all the seeds lying underneath the surface of her, being nourished and loved by her and when the time is right, they start unfolding and growing. Through her support, they find the courage to grow and flourish.

Whenever I tune into the energy of the Great Mother, I feel a sense of total love. Her ability to nurture and allow you to feel supported and loved is immense. I do however find, as a Starseed, I often feel disconnected from her and her gifts. As a collective we have forgotten how to listen to her love and guidance. During this work, please remember that you have chosen to be here and work with her energy. Open your heart to her again.

This is the foundation for us to start our work with the Star energy. Unless we are fully grounded and connected to Mother Gaia, we only experience a fraction of the magic of the Stars. The more you connect with Gaia the more you connect with the Cosmos.

THE SHADOW DESIRE

The shadow within means different things to people, so here again is how I work with this concept in this process. For me it represents the parts of me that are hidden. Some of it is glorious and some not so glorious. But within each and every one there are parts that want to be seen and heard. Often these parts of us are buried as a response to people or events in our lives.

When I was a teenager, I was shamed by a bunch of people for not being able to express myself properly and this instilled great fear and judgement within me. I still have visions of people laughing and looking at me like I was crazy. This resulted in me taking my voice and my ability to stand up and speak up and I hid it away. I hid it away out of fear. Fear of being judged and laughed at again. Fear of failing again. I used the Sacred Circle to reclaim my voice.

Here are some examples of parts of you that you might have hidden –

YOUR VOICE

> always being told to be quiet or that what you want to say is not valid or does not matter, not being heard by those closest to you.

YOUR IDEAS

people around you did not listen or invalidated your thoughts and ideas.

YOUR SENSITIVITY

you are too sensitive, stop being so emotional.

YOUR CREATIVITY

your creative expression was not accepted or made smaller and invalid.

YOUR WEIRDNESS

you should behave more normal like everyone else, you need to fit in.

YOUR BOUNDARIES

you should stop being selfish. What does everyone else need?

YOUR POWER

you are too much, tone yourself down.

There are loads of other examples, but these are a start to allow you to connect with what you are hiding. If any of these examples made you go YES inside of you, please take note. If anything in this list above made your body feel uncomfortable please take note, it matters. Your body is talking to, and your Soul speaks through your body.

Often this part of us that we are hiding is the part that wants to be heard, seen, or experienced the most. That is a key to your authentic self-expression. If more than one of the list items showed up for you, take a moment, take a deep breath and ask yourself which one feels like it wants to be worked with right now. We always work with one concept at a time.

Your Soul desires the hidden part to be shown again because part of your most magical self lies there.

THE NORTH MEDITATION

To start off our work I will be asking you to listen to the North meditation at the following link – **www.divinesoul.me/meditations**

Once you have listened to the meditation please start on the work below and let's delve deeper into you, your shadow and desires.

Please don't try and start the work if you haven't listened to the meditation.

The meditation connects you with the energy of Mother Gaia and gives you more clarity on the shadow desire that you can work with in this section of the book.

Please also note that you can keep coming back to this part of the book whenever you feel like you need it. Our shadow desires are constantly popping up. New parts of us want to be seen all the time, so we need to allow that. This process is designed to help you unravel more and more.

SHADOW DESIRE CLARITY

Write down the shadow desire that you were shown during the meditation. Remember, a single word is all you need. You don't yet need to understand it or even worry about fixing it. We are taking this one step at a time. Take your journal and write down the first word that you were given in our meditation. And PLEASE – don't let your mind get involved here. It doesn't matter what it was, how trivial or silly you might think this word is, it is really relevant, and it matters to unravel the concept behind it. So let's get going!

1

First, we need to connect with the feeling of the shadow desire. When you think of this shadow right now as it stands, as the hidden, scared and unseen part of you - what does it feel like? I want you to close your eyes, take three deep breaths in very slowly. Put all your attention to your breath, see it moving in and out of your body. Then once you can feel yourself calm and your body calm, I want you to think and imagine this hidden shadow.

> Where in your body is it feeling tense? Your stomach, your heart, your back?
>
> What does it feel like, tight, sore, anxious, overwhelmed?

Whatever you are feeling in your body is right for you, there is no wrong here.

Note this feeling down in your journal, as this is the way that shadow presents in your physical being. By understanding it, when you feel that sensation going forward you know the shadow is presenting itself. You want to get to know that feeling, make friends with it and face it. Awareness is power.

I use the example of me finding my voice again here – so when I think about that hidden part of me, I feel it in my solar plexus, the space just under my ribs. I feel anxious and restricted in my body when this fear shows itself to me. I am now able to tune into it, and I immediately know what is happening inside of me. My shadow is requiring my attention and my acknowledgement. Think of this as you getting to know your hidden parts. It's a bit like meeting an old friend.

2

We now want to understand where this shadow shows up in your life. Where is it making an impact and holding you back? I love to use mind maps and I have included an example of my mind map for you below. We use the following areas to focus on:

Family
Career
General Life
Spiritual Growth
Finances
Health

Start writing down anything in those various areas of your life that is impacted by you hiding this part of yourself. Again, for me hiding my voice had a huge impact in my overall life.

Allow yourself to write whatever comes up for you. Again, there is no right or wrong here. We are merely trying to look deeper. So take a few deep breaths and create a mind map or simply just start writing what is coming up for you.

Here is my example, so take some inspiration and guidance from the following:

3

When you think back – when was the first time you felt this feeling? Often, we don't necessarily know where the shadow comes from, but we do know that it is present in our lives. So I have made the connection that finding my voice again was linked to an incident in this life, but when I looked deeper I also found various Past Lives where it showed up.

If you take this shadow desire of yours that you have looked at. What do you think it is trying to teach you in this lifetime? What does it want you to see and acknowledge?

4

Take time to unravel how you feel about this shadow – how is it making you feel? How do you actually like having it in your life? We might think we don't want this 'negative' thing in our life, but subconsciously it is keeping us safe and protected. Think honestly about how it is serving you staying in the shadow. Write this all down.

For me not sharing my voice meant that I was safe. No-one could judge me because I wasn't visible, and I could not judge myself for messing up again. So all was perfectly fine, as far as I was concerned. BUT inside of me my voice was desperate to be shared and I was denying my Soul the opportunity to speak and be heard.

Remember to be very honest with yourself during this whole process. You will know when you are bullshitting yourself here, so stay real and raw!

Once you have completed the work above, take some time to allow this all to integrate. You might find that some more aspects and ideas want to show themselves to you. You have now allowed yourself to open up some deep parts of you, so integration is always important.

I also want to make it very clear that you are not fixing anything or healing anything at this point. We are simply stepping into awareness of our shadow desires. And that is perfect for right now.

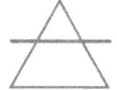

THE EAST

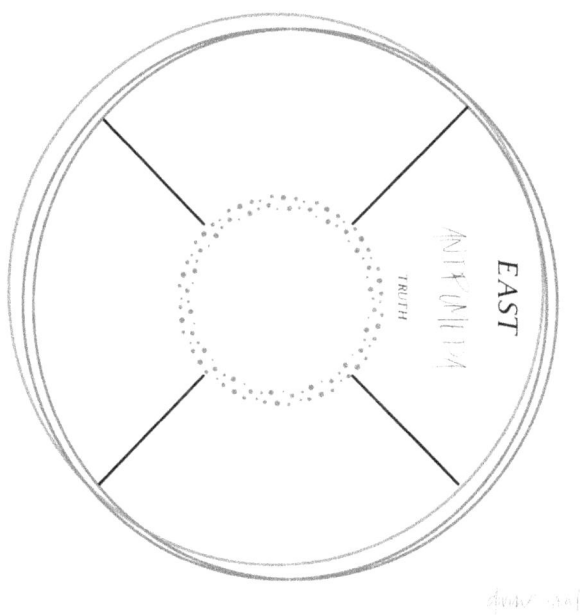

The second direction that we focus on is the East. This is the second point in working with the Starseed Sacred Circle. This part of the Circle is about finding your own inner truth and becoming the warrior that embraces the energy of your own truth.

Through your work in the North, you discovered your hidden shadow desire, you understood where it comes from and how that shadow and non-acceptance of that part of you has the potential to stop you from aligning to your Soul. The journey now starts to uncover what your truth is - who am I and what do I believe?

As we grow up, we are all given a set of rules by our parents and society. These rules and guidelines depend heavily on your circumstances, religion and country. Each of us has a specific pair of glasses that we look through – that is how we see the world.

My question to you is – have you ever taken those glasses off and scrutinised the prescription? We take so many beliefs, values and rules for granted. What we do in this section of the book is start looking at why you believe what you believe. We start delving deeper into who you actually are, and we put a spotlight on parts of you that might not be in alignment with your Soul.

In this section we will be working with the energy of the Andromedan Star Nation and tap into our inner warrior for our own truth.

ANDROMEDAN ENERGIES

Working with the Andromedan energy is the opposite of working with the energy of Mother Gaia. Gaia is a nurturing, loving and cocooning feminine energy. When I connect with the Andromedans, things shift more to the masculine energy and I connect with the Air element. This element is connected to the mind, wisdom and the Soul. It gives you wings, and the ability to start looking at things from that higher perspective. It represents spiritual faith. It reminds you that there is much more out there than you can see, and how you could allow yourself to grow and change, just like the force and direction of wind and air.

When I work with the Andromedan energy it represents courage – courage to embrace change and explore the unknown. As a Star Nation, they are keen explorers and optimistic beings that embrace change and want to assist and make a difference. They strive for freedom, the freedom to express and to be real. So if you ever connect with Andromedans (like myself) here on Earth, then you will see our greatest driver is freedom and connection to authentic expression. We also hold a deep courage within. Fiercely fighting for equality and the truth.

The Andromedan energy is also deeply connected to the rising of the Divine Feminine energy here on Earth. Even though the Andromedan energy feels more masculine and goal oriented, the freedom lies in balance. You will see the fierce support from them to bring back the balance between the Divine Feminine and the Divine Masculine. Supporting the emergence of joy, beauty and balance again. And all of this can only be achieved if we know our own truth.

FINDING YOUR TRUTH

Your Soul holds a deep truth. Your Soul wants to express and experience that truth here on this Earth. Part of the process of expanding our consciousness is to understand who we are. I always return to the inscription at the temple in Delphi – 'Know Thyself'.

I grew up in a Christian household and we went to church every Sunday and my beliefs for the first 20 years of my life were very much governed by the dogma of the Church. I then started questioning this as I became a teenager and by the time I was 20, I stopped going to church. I spent most of my 20s floating around, trying to decipher my truth and after my son was born in my early 30s, I started delving deeper. A book on Past Lives set my world on fire and changed everything for me. I finally found the missing pieces and started reading like crazy trying to understand more about concepts and ideas that I never heard about. Then when the shift in my career happened from business analyst to Akashic Record reader, I had to clarify many beliefs and open my mind even more.

My responsibility was to keep an open mind and see what I would see in the Akashics without placing my own beliefs and filters on the messages I had to give my clients. I chose to leave the belief system that was instilled by my family and my society behind to rather pursue my own truth. This was not easy and I still have family members and friends who don't agree with my choices and how I show up in the world.

BUT it is okay. It is not for them to choose how I express myself. It is my job to align to my Soul truth. To get to this point took a lot of healing of my people-pleasing aspects and my fears around judgement. It is a work in progress, but I just keep getting better at setting my boundaries here.

Have you sat yourself down and done a bit of an inventory of your ideas and beliefs? I am going to share a couple of questions with you and want you to take a moment to answer them truthfully. I also want you to think why you believe what you believe. Did this come from your parents, society or is this from you? Again, there is no right or wrong. There is only what feels good within you and opens up your heart.

So answer these questions from your heart and let's see what you find.

> Do you believe in a god / higher power / source / Divine?
>
> Do you believe in the Soul having a purpose?
>
> Why are you here?

> Who are you without the labels of wife, husband, partner, mother, father, brother, sister or child?
>
> Who are you without the labels of your day job?
>
> Who do you want to be?

Once you have answered these, think about how you are showing up in the world and supporting your beliefs. Do those close to you and around you know what you believe or are you hiding it away? Why are you hiding it away?

Often, we wear masks to stop us from getting hurt or judged by those around us. Are you wearing a mask?

If I am doing anything in my life that is not authentic, I am not in alignment with my Soul.

If you are forcing yourself to do things from a space of obligation, shame or guilt – you need to look at it. Your Soul does not lead from the word 'should.'

And you know what – you technically don't even have to show up for your own Soul, you can just stay on the couch and stare at your phone and be. That is perfect too by the way!

But be warned, she is forever whispering, stirring and prodding us. And I can choose to ignore it, but deep inside I know the truth about being here. I know that I have chosen to come here and to experience my truth authentically.

And I guess the fact that you are reading this, shows me you aren't staying on the couch – I write with a smile on my face!

THE EAST MEDITATION

To answer the next set of questions please ensure that you first listen to the East meditation at the following link – **www.divinesoul.me/meditations**

This meditation leads you back to a part of you that you have forgotten and shows you a truth about yourself. Make time to listen and then answer the set of questions below.

QUESTIONING YOUR TRUTH

When I start to look at who I really am versus what I have been conditioned to believe, I start to see my inauthentic parts showing up. Those parts of me where I am behaving in ways that keep others happy and comfortable. The way to my inner truth is through authenticity.

Take some time now to answer the following questions:

> Where in your life are you currently being authentic?
>
> Where do you show up in your truest colours? Where do you show up as yourself with no judgement?

In which areas of your life are you not showing up as yourself:

> Family
> Work
> Friends
> Social Media

What are you hiding from them?

What would you love people to know or see about you?

Why are you so scared of showing this to them?

What do you believe will happen if they see these parts of you?

Now that you have honestly answered these questions, do you see any pattern? Do you see places in your life that are highlighted as spaces of not being real?

My conscious understanding of these behaviours points me to places and parts of myself that want to emerge and that I am hiding. I also know that these parts of you have been wounded in the past, and that they need healing. And it isn't always just a case of getting over ourselves and moving through stuff. I am not here to support victim mentality, but I am here to support compassion.

We are all in the process of learning to take responsibility for our own shit. For the stuff that we have chosen to hide. And this can feel hard and painful and heavy. But with all this, we move down to one single point. It is the point of making a choice.

You, and only you, can choose how to proceed. You can choose to be courageous and make a choice to help you heal or you can choose to stay on the couch and watch the world pass you by.

I am here to show you that by healing your wounds and allowing yourself to become more authentic each and every day, you step closer to your Soul. You step closer to a life of contentment, acceptance, allowance and peace. And you know what, when I create and live from that space I fill the world with love!

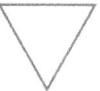

THE SOUTH

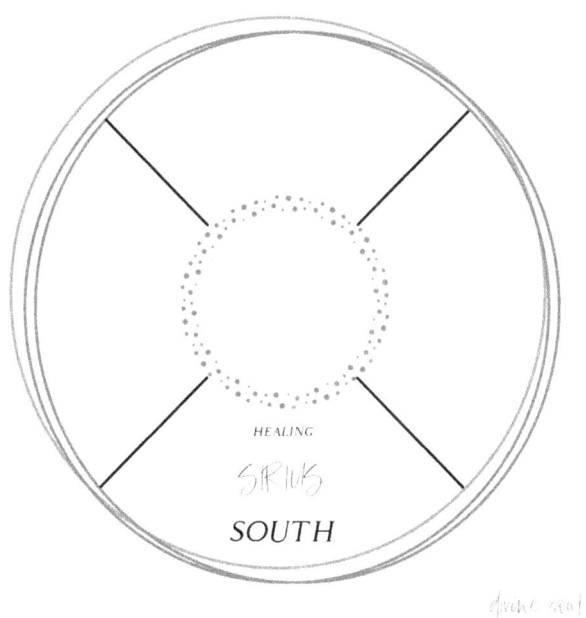

The third direction that we focus on is the South. This is the third point in working with the Starseed Sacred Circle. During our time in the East, we worked with understanding our deeper truth, seeing where we are not aligned with our Soul and starting to feel into what needs healing within.

When you start seeing your truth and you start seeing the obstacles that are stopping you from connecting to it, the healing can begin. So during the next part of our journey I want to show you how to clearly and honestly look at what you need to heal right now.

As I am sitting here writing, the radio blaring in the background, I can hear the singer say – 'It only takes one match to burn a thousand trees…' (Thousand Trees by Stereophonics). And that is our healing journey – it only takes one match to burn down what is holding you back. In our old paradigm of healing, we used to be attached to years of trying to heal and release old patterns and wounds. But now as we have entered this beautiful new age of Aquarius, time has sped up, the energies are supporting our journeys of acceleration and expansion. So see this part of the journey as an invitation to let go.

Once we let go of the resistance, we allow flow to happen. This direction is connected to water and flow. A beautiful feminine energy of healing and nurturing. So allow yourself to be gentle and compassionate during this process.

Letting go takes courage. The fact that you are brave enough to be honest about your truth means that you can be brave enough to trust that flow can return. Often we want to hold on to our old ways of being because we can't see how we can be any other way. But what if I told you that the most liberating and expansive thing that you can ever do for yourself is to let go and trust?

When you find yourself sitting here right now looking into your future, can you start imagining what it would be like if there was no resistance within you?

During our journey in the South we work with the energy of Sirius.

SIRIUS ENERGIES

Sirius is the brightest Star in our sky. Sirius A is the bright star and then there is Sirius B a dwarf star that orbits around Sirius A every 50 years. Long before our modern technology showed us Sirius B, the shadow star, the ancients knew about its existence. As far back as 3,000 years ago, there were drawings tracking its movements already. Sirius governed the calendars, texts and sacred knowledge of the ancients – think Lemuria, Atlantis, Sumer, Egypt, Africa, Australia, South America and Asia.

Sirius is also associated with various power animals here on Earth – the White Lions are said to be connected with Sirius and the African Shamans love working with this energy as it is bringing renewal to the continent. Then there is also the connection with dolphins – the keepers of joy and love and so many amazing light codes. Sirius is also connected with the Whales – the keepers of the Akashic Records.

In ancient times, Sirius was the indicator of fertility. It was the time when the ancients knew that the rivers would flood and bring water to much needed areas which would provide sustenance and wealth for many. So when I connect with the energy of Sirius it always feels like a creator of the new. It ends off the energy of the old and connects us with potential and possibility.

Taking us out of a state of war to a state of peace. Taking us out of a state of judgement back into a state of love and acceptance. Creating again the beautiful balance between the masculine and feminine energies within each of us.

When I work with Sirius Starseeds there is an air of practicality and purpose. Making things better is always a theme. The energies from them are on point and have this feeling of, 'Let's get going. There is lots to do and we need to get this done'. So for me it made so much sense when the Sirians showed me that they wanted to be part of the healing journey of the Sacred Circle – moving us through our own judgements and the judgements of others back to love and acceptance. And when we have entered that space, we create from there.

OBSERVATION

During your journey through the Circle we have worked with finding your shadow desire. And then in the journey through your truth, you were able to identify where you weren't fully in your truth because of judgement. This is how I identify my wounds. I see where judgement comes up and that links me straight back to my own wounds. By seeing what I am hiding from myself and others, I go back to my wounds. My observation and analysis of my wounds is such a great step towards healing myself.

I remember when I first started my Akashic Record reading business, I did not speak about it on my personal Facebook page and was living what I would call a double life. I had one group of friends who knew me as 'normal' Yolandi and then there was the 'weird' Yolandi friends. This created a lot of anxiety for me as I was constantly trying to not be seen as 'weird' by the other people in my life.

I was visiting friends that I had not seen for a couple of years. They knew me from school days and somehow my friend's wife had found out that I was now doing this new work. My friend was shocked but also asked me to tell them more about what I was doing and how it worked. We ended up having an extremely long conversation about my work, with genuine curiosity from both of them and no judgement. They thought it was super strange that I had changed my view on life so much, but they also knew me as a person enough to see my intentions for my work and how I wanted it to help people.

So what is my point here? Well, often we perceive that people are going to freak out or do something crazy when they hear about your truth, but sometimes you will be pleasantly surprised to find out that even though they don't necessarily agree with it they will respect your decision. I must add that the same friend eventually ended up getting a reading from me, so that was pretty amazing too.

If you have experienced the other side of this coin, though, and been thrown into the deep dark pool of judgement by someone that you love, then let's look at it from a higher perspective. The person that you told your truth to, holds their own truth. Just like you, they have gone through life wearing their own set of glasses and now you are shaking their world and questioning their set of glasses. You might be triggering an unseen wound or truth within them by sharing this part of yourself. If we take the time to understand where people come from, especially those that oppose our truth then it puts our issues into a different perspective. Very often their response might be from a place of ignorance or conditioning or wounding.

If you have ever read, *The Four Agreements* by Don Miguel Ruiz you will know about the one agreement that says, 'Don't take anything personally'. I love this piece of advice and wisdom and this has truly changed my life and the way that I look at other people. So put that hurt and judgement that they put on you and work your way backwards, go back to their pain and if you can't pinpoint it, at least be in the space of knowing that there is a deep wound there that is not because of you.

And this is where empathy comes into play. When I can start to understand and feel the pain in those who have harmed me or judged me, I can stand back and create a space of deep understanding. When I can see that often they don't actually know how to act any differently, I can start forgiving and letting go.

Having read this now, take a moment to look at that fear that you carry with you about living and sharing your truth. Our hearts are often full of hurt and scars because of the judgement of others and our own judgement towards ourselves.

So looking back at the information you have gathered about yourself thus far, answer a few of these questions:

What does the judgement of others/myself show me about myself?

Am I willing to risk my authentic truth for what others are thinking or saying about me?

Why is it so important for me to be liked or loved by those whom I see judging me?

Can I see the higher perspective around their judgement?

What would change if I chose today to start loving myself?

What would change if I chose to forgive myself?

Once you have answered these questions we can proceed to the meditation and go and connect with the beautiful loving beings of Sirius to help us heal our wounds and start opening our hearts to Divine Love again.

THE SOUTH MEDITATION

Take some time out now to listen to the South Meditation at the following link –
www.divinesoul.me/meditations

Once you have completed the meditation, allow yourself to just be in that feeling of love and softness for a little while. The healing energies from Sirius are like a sweet nectar that wants to fill our entire being, so allow yourself some time there before starting the next section of our journey.

EXPECTATIONS

The energies of the South are focusing on healing ourselves and letting go of our patterns – by being in awareness of our wounds and releasing expectations that keeps putting us back into our wound patterns. I add this section in here so you can pay attention to what keeps cropping up for you. Expectations have the ability to put you in an endless loop.

When I look at the concept of expectations, I start with what I think others are expecting of me and how I think they want me to behave or show up in our interactions. Very seldom have any of the people in my life expressed these expectations that I think they have of me. So here is a simple example. About six years ago, I started travelling around the world by myself. The husband and I made an agreement that we both would get time out from the family and each other, so we usually have a two to three week annual policy and you get to do whatever you choose all by yourself. The reason for this is that we both have interests that the other one does not share, for him it is cycling really, really far and for me it is sacred site exploration. And I can't imagine Rob at some Mary Magdalene retreat somewhere or meditating on Machu Picchu. As much as I love watching the dot of his bike move across different parts of the planet, he needs his adventures of exploring the world on his bicycle.

So when we started this way of being, I would be off on a two week retreat and I would make sure everything was organised, Ben would have little gift boxes and me phoning every day and checking in. Making sure that they would not notice I was not there and that I could in turn feel less guilty for taking time out for myself and pursing adventures that mattered to me. The husband, on the other hand, would get on a plane, kiss us goodbye, phone every few days and do his thing. And then one day a few years in, the husband turned to me and asked why I was always making such a big fuss about going away. He is quite capable of going to the shop, buying food and looking after our son without me.

Here I was with this expectation that I created, thinking that they were both expecting me to do all these things, but they never even asked for it. They did not even think it was required, but I believed that it was necessary because I felt guilty for leaving, for not being the doting mommy and wife who had to be home looking after my family.

And I realised that I was creating expectations. I was imagining they needed this from me and they didn't. Creating those expectations fuelled my anxiety, fuelled my guilt and lead to me forever worrying about finding a time to speak to my family every day whilst I was supposed to be enjoying myself. So I stopped. And now when I am on my world travels I phone when I miss them or when the time is right, not out of obligation or guilt. Realising that I was allowed to have time and space for me was a biggie, and now I claim it and I relish it.

So where are you creating expectations? How many of the things and the people that you worry about every single day are you creating in your head? Have they ever asked you for what you think they are expecting of you?

One of the biggest hurdles in healing yourself is to let go of what you imagine others are expecting of you. To let go of how you imagine they are judging you.

Take stock of where you keep looping on these expectations and judgements. Sit down and try to remember if they have ever actually asked or commented in a way that you think they have. Or is this your wounding showing itself again?

My woundings above were the guilt about not being a good enough mother and wife. But neither my husband or child have ever told me that I am not meeting their expectations. The only thing they really expected of me was love, and that I gave in bucket loads already, so none of the other things were required or expected. They had no judgement within their hearts, only I held judgement of myself.

THE HEALING JOURNEY

Healing my wounds is an ongoing process and journey. When I started this work, I did not realise how complex we are as human beings, and that there is always something new to discover about myself. I always think of myself as a human full of scars. But each scar is a memory about how I overcame some obstacle, learnt something new, or started loving myself more.

I can choose to hold onto my wounds and live my life from that story. And I know I have done that before, but I have also learnt that it holds me back. It stops me from discovering amazing new things about myself and it stops me from moving towards new places and parts of myself that my Soul wants to show me. I choose to let go of being a victim and living in victim consciousness.

It is always about choice. You have to decide if you want to replay this old record or do you want to release yourself, set yourself free?

And each time you set yourself free from an old wound, your heart opens a little more to the magic of the Universe and life. You see yourself from a new perspective and you get to love yourself a little more each day.

Remember these spirals keep showing up, there is always a little more healing to do somewhere. As you have journeyed through this part of the Circle with me, what other wounds have you started to become aware of? Make note of what else is coming up for you here as it might be important for you to revisit this again and unravel anything else that you have noticed about yourself here.

Your wounds are so beautiful and so important, so make sure that you keep looking at them, loving them and accepting them. They will bring you back to you.

THE WEST

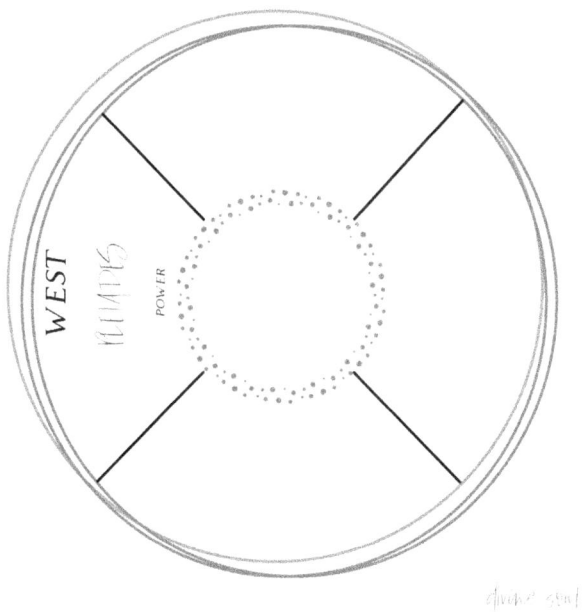

The fourth direction that we focus on is the West. Whilst working with this part of the wheel we move into the area of power. Up until now you have worked with the shadow aspects of yourself, understanding your truth and healing the judgements that you carry. Now it is time to embrace the powerful, mystical aspect of the self. That part of you that wants to step into your power. The desire that your Soul has already shown you on our journey together.

Power is such an interesting part of our journey to discover. It is something that can be taken away from you or something that you choose to give away.

When we start analysing Past Lives, it is clear to see if a person chose to give away their power or had it taken away from them. I would often see that choosing to give power away is linked to feelings of judgement, hopelessness, and lack of worth or self-belief. BUT as always, a choice was made in that life to avoid an uncomfortable situation and the easier option was to give power away.

I have seen in my own life the situations where I chose to give my power away. In my case, it was very clear in my relationships how this played out.

In my younger years I always lost myself somewhere along the way, trying to keep men in my life, or trying to make them love me or stay with me. After meeting my now husband, it took me a long time of healing my own internal issues with self-worth. We started our relationship from a place of extreme truth. Having both come out of failed marriages, we chose to show up with all our ugly bits exposed. We shared our deepest darkest secrets and chose to not be in judgement of each other. It was the first time in my life where I could show up as my real but also broken self. He supported me in my healing journey and when those horrible moments of extreme insecurity arose in our relationship, he was there. And the more I healed those aspects of myself, the stronger I became, the more I became my own person, moving into my truth and worth every day. The more I healed, the better our relationship got and the more the power struggles disappeared. And balance in our relationship returned and I took my power back.

The same theme played out in my other relationships. It was always about being good enough, being a complete people-pleaser and always wanting to save everyone around me.

In my corporate career, I was always killing myself. I would be the one working till crazy hours of the night, fixing things, trying to make it all work so that the team would be seen and be acknowledged. I always out-performed wherever I was, so that I would keep my bosses happy, cover up messes for people in the teams so they would not get into trouble. Always putting my hand up for all the projects.

Until I started to understand how being this chameleon that needed to change to keep everyone happy and to make sure that they loved me was eroding my truth and my own power.

And this, once again, would come down to my favourite little word – judgement!

Giving my power away to all of those countless unhealthy relationships in my past was another way that I was avoiding judgement. Another way that I was avoiding healing my wounds and showing up as my true self.

And the biggest lesson over these many years was that if I am in a healthy relationship with myself it is reflected right back at me. Healthy boundaries, taking my needs into consideration and not being in fear of judgement, saved me. My deepest relationships are the ones where I allow myself to show my shadows and my truths.

So how are you showing up in your relationships? Are you in your truth?

When I stepped more into my truth and healed my fears and judgements, my power wanted to come out and play. She was ready to be lit up again and to show herself to the world.

Fire and power feel so intertwined. Fire represents rebirth for me. I always think of this plant called Fynbos in South Africa and these plants actually need fire in order for the seed pods to heat up and release new seeds that can grow. So I see it as heating up my centre with the fire and then allowing all the beautiful seeds to sprout out so they can be sown and I can tend to them.

When I am in my truth, the light inside burns brighter. The brighter it burns the more I shine, the more I shine, the more I am truly in my own power again.

But I am also aware of fire being a very destructive element, and if I leave it unattended it can wreak havoc and destroy. Balance is required when working with our own internal flame and power.

PLEIADIAN ENERGIES

The Pleiadians are beautiful beings here to help us with the spiritual evolution on Earth. Pleiadian Souls are here to assist the world with change. There are currently millions of Souls carrying Pleiadian energy incarnated here on this earth. They are visionaries, teachers and communicators. These Souls are not afraid of change and will make things happen. Their ability to see the big picture is amazing and they inspire those around them to want to change. They really just need a little help with the practicalities of implementing those grand visions here into reality. So if you identify with being a Pleiadian, make sure you surround yourself with awesome teams to build those beautiful dreams that you hold for humanity.

The ancients also connected with the Pleiades and in various texts and channellings it is mentioned that this Soul Group helped with seeding the planet right at the beginning of it all and the DNA creation of humankind as we know it today.

They were also involved in the eras of Atlantis and Lemuria and connected to many channelled methods of energy healing over the years. Their presence here on Earth now is playing a very important role in shifting our truths around mystical elements, ancient wisdom and the knowledge that we hold. They are also assisting us in working more with the energies of the different Star Nations. Reminding us again of our own divinity, our connection to the Divine and the collective consciousness.

I am always very grateful that they showed up for me when I was going through the process of finding my power again. One of my most amazing visions was of them waiting for me on top of a very big Aztec pyramid. I had to climb to the top after having walked through pits of snakes. I knew they were waiting and during the vision I could see them but I had to overcome many obstacles to get to them. And as I reached the top of the pyramid they showed me a big book that was still closed. They told me about the date when they would open the book for me and how I would then be able to work with new energies and bring new information into the world. On the date that they showed me a few years ago, I went into ceremony with my Soul Sisters and we started opening up new portals of information and light. I haven't looked back since then and am forever grateful to them as they showed me my potential, and other things that I saw in the vision that day are still unfolding and being understood even now.

They show us our potential and help us to step into who we are at a Soul level.

POWER PLAY

What is your definition of power and do you think of yourself as a powerful person?

When you start understanding what it means to you to be powerful, it changes many things. It is one of those phrases that is thrown around a lot out there. Stepping into your power, embodying your power, becoming your most powerful self…

But each and every one of us holds a truth around power and this is always my starting point for self-exploration. So what is my truth around power and what does it mean to me?

Well, here goes – being in my power means to be the most authentic version of myself that I am currently capable of and constantly striving to be more of who I feel and know I am deep inside. Sometimes being in my power means getting out of bed and rocking the day. Other times being in my power means curling up on the sofa and binge-watching Netflix. My power does not like judgement, my power loves compassion and my power loves explosive ideas and running with them like I am on fire. She sits in the centre of my chest, she feels expansive and open and filled with possibility, but she also feels like a little fire in my solar plexus and sometimes she burns hotter and sometimes a little less. Sometimes I feel a bit overwhelmed by her, but I am intrigued by how it feels, so I am always curiously exploring more and trying to see more. Giving that part of me freedom.

My power is a complex being, but she is honest and real. She is not afraid to show the world when she is on the floor sobbing or when she is soaring like an eagle. My power is the realness and truth that I crave in the world.

So here are some questions I would love for you to consider:

What does your power look like?

What does your power feel like in your body?

Are you living in your power right now?

Who are you giving your power away to right now? Think about boundaries here, feelings of guilt and obligation towards some people.

Who are you allowing to take your power away? Where do you feel helpless and powerless in a relationship?

What are you really afraid of? Be honest here, we all have fears. Mine is of failure, so what is yours?

The more aware that I am of my fear the easier it is for me to be in my power. So how does that work? Well, I've said this before, awareness is power. Awareness is the key to navigating through my shadows and my fears. When I can step back and see what I am afraid of and move myself out of the emotions and become the observer of my actions and feelings, I can choose objectively. Breathing and taking my time to sit with it, helps me to understand it, and then I can make a choice that connects me again to my truth and in turn to my power.

So those people that you mentioned above, take some time to sit with them, observe your relationship with them. Also observe what you are afraid of or why you are allowing them to treat you a certain way. And it is important that you understand what it is that you actually like about giving your power away or having it taken away.

I know that is a weird thing to say, but hear me out. When I was in that space of giving my power away to other people, what I like to call my people-pleasing phase in life, I secretly liked to be the one who was always helping and saving. Why? Because there was a sense of worth there, a sense of being seen and recognised for the good that I was doing. Deep down inside if I really think about it, it was about me craving that attention that I got for always helping. So what does that feel like within you?

When I unlearned the people-pleasing, I had to find other ways of feeling worthy and that came from understanding myself more, accepting myself more and becoming more of who I was without judgement. And now when I help others, I do so because I want to, not because I need to.

So take a moment to sit with your power and be honest with yourself about where you find yourself at this point in time. This is your starting point for stepping into the meditation with me. Be honest about where you are at and how you feel.

THE WEST MEDITATION

Take some time out now to listen to the West Meditation at the following link –
www.divinesoul.me/meditations

Once you have completed the meditation, allow yourself to just be in the moment. Make some notes in your journal about what came up for you, once you felt the energies that were arising with you.

EMBODIMENT

The Oxford dictionary definition:

> embodiment
> /ɪmˈbɒdɪmənt/
> *noun*
> a tangible or visible form of an idea, quality, or feeling.

I so love that! A tangible form of a feeling. So that is power right there. Power is a feeling that I hold within and that is what I make tangible or visible in my life.

So when I am in my power, I embody the feeling of realness and authenticity. It is not about being strong or being out there like Wonder Woman saving the world. Although I am not going to lie, I would totally love to be her. It is about having the courage each day to show up in my own life in a way that is real. That is the most powerful thing I can do. And for me I can see very clearly that by doing this, people notice. The amount of messages that I get from people thanking me for being brave and being out there warms my heart. It confirms to me that even though I am not on a huge stage somewhere world famous, my embodiment of my power matters and it helps and inspires.

So by choosing to be brave, and believe me most of the time I am shaking in my boots when I do something new or something that requires me to be fully seen, it inspires. So if you choose today to embody your realness who could you inspire?

I was recently a co-author in a book called Living Life Goddess Powered and I wrote about finding my voice and how I lost it in High School. My 12 year old son asked me if he could read it. After he read it, he thanked me for telling the story and he said that he will remember to keep talking and sharing his voice. And that for me was enough. The fact that I can inspire my son to speak his truth is honestly enough. Job done.

Us inspiring those around us, our families, our loved ones, our friends. Job done.

You inspiring one person to be closer to their own truth, they inspire one other person to be closer to their own truth, and they inspire another and so we go on and on and on… Can you see what you can achieve? That is power.

FEARLESS

The idea of being fearless is another interesting concept to work with when it comes to power. And this is something that I struggled with for quite a while.

So logic would dictate that to be in your power you need to be fearless. Well, at least that was what my brain wanted me to believe. I could only be fully in my power if I transcended all fear and was fully healed, fully dealt with all my shadows and 100% in my truth. I literally believed that I had to be perfect, to be in my power.

Over the years, as I delved deeper into this belief, I realised that this was yet another way my ego was stopping me from embodying my power. It was another set of obstacles that I needed to overcome before I was good enough to be in my power. Surprise! Another judgement theme running for me.

But my truth now is that I embody my power, carrying my fears around with me. All my flaws, imperfections and emotional baggage come with me too. All these parts of me are valid. Every single one of them, the good, the bad and the ugly. They all come with me every day.

Fearless to me means to fear less. So even though I am not perfect or without fear, I choose to show up. I choose to speak and I choose to be in my truth. Even though, most of the time, I have enough lavender essential oil on my palms to calm an army down, I am still scared. When my heart is in my throat when I have to start speaking and I secretly would prefer to run away very quickly, I show up.

Those moments of fear remind me that I am human, and you know what they last all of three minutes and then they dissipate as my Soul steps in to take over. My human just has to be there having organised the platform to speak from and then my amazing Soul sweeps in like a super hero and takes over and speaks from that deep place of love and wisdom within me.

Elizabeth Gilbert in her amazing book Big Magic, wrote about fear riding in the car with her – how it had a seat and was part of the family but it never got a vote. This always stuck with me, because we can't get rid of it. The fear is going to be there and it wants to be seen.

But the big difference comes in if you allow it to debilitate you. If you allow it to keep you in the corner or in the closet, hiding away from being seen for who you truly are. So acknowledging it, seeing your humanness become so real when it shows up, is part of your journey here. It is okay to be scared! But do it all anyways. Show up and be you anyways.

I have shed bucket loads of tears and fought very hard with my Soul over the last 10 years about showing up. But I can never win that battle and I am still learning every day how to surrender to her. I know within me there is a power that burns. I also know that within each and every one of us there is a power that burns. And we can try and dowse that flame with all sorts of distractions, with alcohol, with food, with social media, with pain, with fear, with resentment, with obligation, with whatever excuse you have to not try and find your true self. But it is there and it is burning if you like it or not.

And allowing yourself to lie back into that feeling of the flame, feeling the warmth, the support and the potential, that is my idea of heaven. Those moments when I let go of it all and I know that my Soul has got my back and she is here always patiently waiting for my humanness to be with her, those are bliss.

That is stepping into my power, or shall I rather say falling into my power.

THE CENTER

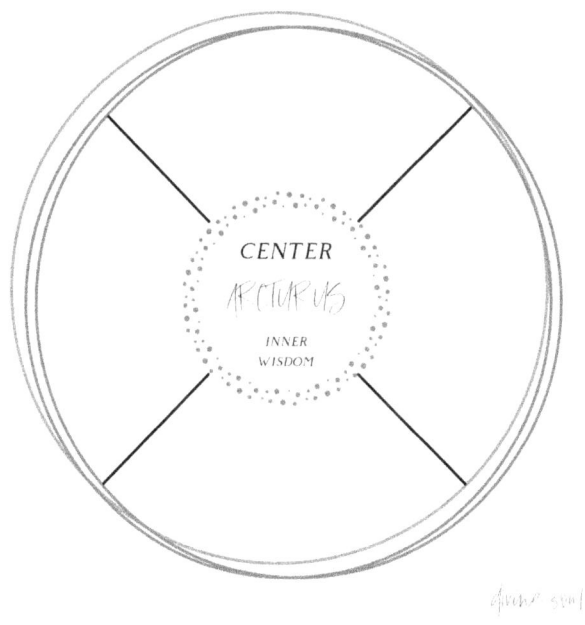

Now that you have journeyed through the four cardinal directions of the Sacred Circle, you come to the Center. You have moved through your shadows, looked at your deepest desires. You wrestled with your truth and chose to see yourself for who you are. You dove deep into healing those parts of you that you judge and worked with accepting yourself deeper. And then you got to the yummy part of playing with your power, understanding what it means to you and how you want to show up in your power in the world. So pulling all of these pieces of you together now we come to the point of connecting to our own inner wisdom.

Deep within each of us lies the Wisdom Keeper. She occupies this sacred space within my being that I have always wanted to get to. She holds this wise knowing, this profound sense of balance and harmony within. Through her words, actions and way of living she inspires those around her to want to find their own inner wisdom.

She shows herself when I am ready to listen. When I realise that I am enough, that I have vision, I am truth, I am not broken and I am powerful. Once I start to understand and own these parts of me, she will step forward. She is always waiting, lurking in the shadows and in the background, she never leaves me. She leads me into expansion, ready for my next journey through the Sacred Circle.

She is the keeper of the I AM energy within me. She is my Soul.

ARCTURIAN ENERGIES

Edgar Cayce the famous Akashic Record prophet described the Arcturians as one of the highest civilisations in our galaxy. They are here to create awareness of our own spiritual wisdom. For me, when I work with the Arcturians, I see them as our teachers and guides. They bring us back to ourselves and show us little bits and pieces of the mysteries that we hold within our energetic being and then help us to start finding our own answers from within ourselves.

I also love working with Arcturian Starseeds here on earth as they have this way of making you go deeper within yourself. They carry this energy of spiritual wisdom through their extremely conscious way of living and being. I find it so inspiring and many of them are sharing their beautiful insights with the world.

I often find them in the background counselling and guiding people and we usually know them as the influencers behind influencers. So if you do identify with being an Arcturian Starseed, please make sure that you share that amazing insight with the world. We need it – it helps us look at things differently and it steers us back to our truths. I know it has done for me.

The Arcturian energies that I love to work with are often linked to teaching us to overcome those human obstacles that we create in this world. These obstacles stop us from the evolution of our own consciousness and in turn this then also affects the evolution of consciousness of the collective. And this is what the Arcturians are most interested in. They acknowledge that we all have the capability to expand and move forward, but the human within us all often chooses to stay small, afraid, divided and disempowered. I think they are a bit baffled by how our emotions and our ability to overthink steer us away from our greatness, as they are just in acceptance of the magnificence of all. So a lot of their work is to remind us of the connectedness of everything in this Universe.

They are trying to teach us about what is beyond this Universe, but they feel that this will take some time as we still need to wrap our heads around the connectedness in this Universe (me imagining them giggling at us).

They are also here to teach us to start enjoying this human and Soul experience. They remind us that it does not have to be as hard as we want to make it. Humans carry this heavy burden of having to save everyone right now, but they are making us aware that our first priority is to just be unapologetically ourselves. That we are here to shine our light the best we can without judgement and that will ignite the changes that we know are needed on our planet.

Being in that vibration of allowing and acceptance is one of the highest vibrations you can carry. Allowing and accepting yourself is real love. So running around the planet in that beautiful vibration of love – imagine what you can achieve. You become an activator of love in others.

They teach us to leave the how at the door and to work with the energy of trust – the knowing that we will be guided to exactly where our light is needed most.

TRUST

At some point along the way we forgot how to trust ourselves fully. Earlier in the book I wrote about starting to listen to our intuition again and how important this is.

The path to owning and recognising my inner wisdom was full of very hard lessons. A few months after my own DNA Activation I hit a brick wall. At that stage I was working with a myriad of coaches all telling me how I should be trying to show up in the world and I was desperately trying to pull all the pieces together. I mean I just had my DNA activated – surely things should be continuing on this upward trajectory but, no, the Universe had another plan for me.

Because things were going so great, I gladly parked my shadow work and decided to ignore it for a while. I chose to go outside of myself and listen to everyone else trying to tell me how to show up in the world. It was such a hard time, even thinking back on it my body aches. The resistance within me was so huge. I just could not sit myself down and look at what I was actually doing. Looking back now I know it was meant to happen so I could learn from it and teach my DNA

Activation clients how to work with their shadows and not just ignore them as I chose to do during that time. The biggest realisation was that I was not trusting myself. I kept going outside of myself for answers, I did not imagine that I could possibly lead myself down this path. There was always someone smarter, more experienced or wiser than me.

But as I was on my knees crying and begging the Universe to take that pain and emptiness away it hit me like a ton of bricks. My Soul was standing there patiently waiting for me to put my hand up and call her in. So I stopped. I stopped all the coaches and teachers and gurus. I went on a self-imposed coach sabbatical and I knew that I first had to come back to myself again.

So once I started making sure that I made time for her, things started shifting. My resistance started melting. I got back into my shadow work and I got back into understanding my fears and judgements. It was amazing. And just like that a few months later the channelling started happening. I was able to go into session with clients and start seeing these amazing messages and images for them. The more I started to trust, the more my consciousness expanded and things started to grow.

That moment of realising that I need to trust me shifted everything.

I can listen to my Soul, I can hear my Soul, I can feel my Soul. She is right here. All it takes is a quiet moment to sit with her and all becomes clearer.

So how much do you trust yourself?

Here are a few questions for you to consider:

> When you need to make a big decision, do you consult others around you?
>
> Do you ever make big life decisions on a whim? If not, why not?
>
> Why do you ask other people their opinions about your decisions?
>
> What would happen if you made a decision by yourself? Will it go wrong?
>
> Have you ever actually made decisions that have gone badly wrong? What was it and why did you choose that option?

When I went through my reliance on all that is outside myself phase – yes I know that is a long name for a phase, but it was a thing as you saw – I was constantly questioning myself. Inside of me it felt like a storm all of the time. I just could not see the wood for the trees most days.

So when I realised what I was busy doing to myself I had to understand what my driving force was for not trusting myself. I needed to whittle it down to something that made sense to me. So when I looked at my inability to make my own decisions, I discovered that I had a very deep seated fear of failure. I know I have been carrying this since childhood and I actually identified the moment of shame when one of the other kids in primary school made fun of me for not coming first in class. The little rebel in me wanted to show him and so I made sure that I would always win and be first. I know my Mom always said she could not understand what drove me so hard and at one stage, she had to step in and tell me to go out and play and stop studying. This really helped and stopped me from completely burning myself out and forgetting to be a kid.

Again, as an adult, I could see this a lot clearer and I even worked this right back to some Past Life events that were still fuelling that fear of failure within me. But all of it came right back to one concept, it came back to judgement AGAIN.

Others judging me for not achieving what I set out to do – making fun of me or something really bad happening because I failed in my quest. I was so astounded by everything returning back to the point of judgement.

So I want you to take a moment and think about the concept of trusting yourself and seeing where does judgement come into play. When making decisions in your life for things that matter to you, where does judgement show up, especially when you worry about failing or making the wrong decision?

If you took away judgement and made decisions from a purely Soul-led perspective what would that feel like? What would your life look like then?

THE CENTER MEDITATION

Take some time out now to listen to the Center Meditation at the following link –
www.divinesoul.me/meditations

Once you have completed the meditation, take a moment to close your eyes and tune into the energy of your Soul. The more we become familiar with what she/he feels like, the more we strengthen the bond and connection. This is again like riding a bike – the more I do it the better I get at it.

YOUR TREASURE CHEST

Have you ever wondered about the word treasure chest – when I saw this the first time I laughed out loud. The word chest jumped out at me. You will always hear me speaking about the center of our chests as our heart portal. The doorway into the unknown. But here is where the treasure lies, in the chest – the treasure chest!

Inside each of us we have so much magic. I see this space in my chest, this dark space as the place where I store my magical parts. Every lifetime that I have had since the initial moment that I came into consciousness has had a little bit of magic and learning. And I take these various bits and I put them into my treasure chest. They become part of my toolbox of wisdom that I can open whenever I need, in whatever lifetime I am in and I can use them to learn and grow more. So as I stand here today I have had some amazing lifetimes behind me, and that in turn means that I have learnt some amazing lessons (good and bad).

Every answer I require is within me. My Soul is the custodian of this information. She is like the librarian who will hand me the right book or tool from the other side of the portal and I can use that to guide myself through this human experience.

The more I learn to trust her and the more I acknowledge and understand that we are in partnership, the easier it will get to ask for the tools and to receive the tools from her.

Building a relationship with your Soul is like any other relationship in your life. You learn to trust that person. You learn to understand them better and to see how they do things. And the only way I get to know someone better is to spend time with them. I don't just instantly know my partner or best friend. It takes time. It takes a lot of honesty and connection for us to deepen our relationships.

So the more time I give to my Soul, the deeper our connection becomes, the clearer the way she communicates with me becomes and the better we work together. This creates more access to my amazing existing treasure chest and the more I get to learn from myself.

OVERWHELM

Those moments of extreme overwhelm where you can't hear yourself or feel into what you need to do, will happen. Losing your connecting with your Inner Wisdom. Feeling like you and your Soul have disconnected happens.

And this is normal. Those are the moments when our humanness becomes too much and our whole ecosystem is thrown out of balance. This is a sign that you need to stop.

You need to stop, take yourself out of your life and the intense buzzing and happening and move into nature. Take yourself for a little sit down, somewhere preferably on bare Mother Earth, root properly connected to the Earth. And start breathing, and breathing and then a little more breathing. If you can place your hands on the ground around you as well and keep breathing. Those negative ions rising from Mother Earth will immediately calm your nervous system down. The extra oxygen will also help immensely. And through this all just keep breathing until you can feel your whole body starting to relax.

I remember a therapist once describing to me what happens with us when we get to these moments of overwhelm. She said it was like a jar filled with water and glitter, if you shake it all the glitter is in the water and it sparkles and it is intense when you look at it and then as you stop shaking the jar the glitter slowly starts drifting to the bottom of the jar and the water becomes clear again. So that is what we basically do to our bodies and minds. Our adrenals are permanently on overdrive as we are rushing through life like bullet trains, needing to finish this and get to that. We don't have space or time to stop and breathe. We forget to breathe.

But when you create space for pause, space for breath and space to be, it all calms down and you can return to your body. Thus, in turn you get to start feeling her talking to you again and your Soul can be heard again.

For me I have this sofa in the corner of our dining room and it looks out over my back garden. It is my place. Seeing that I am in the UK, often it is cold and wet but that space is my breathing space where I can still feel nature and find myself again. No phone or electronics here, just me, some cool crystals that calm me down and the view of nature. But when the sun is out, my garden and sitting on the grass or walking to a forest nearby are my places where I get back to myself, to my breath and to my Soul. My beautiful inner wisdom Soul. In these spaces I can hear and feel myself again, I can guide myself back into alignment again. So find a space for you, your place to breathe yourself back into you. And then you can hear the Soul speak again.

And to be clear here, sometimes we need to do this a lot! We need to stop a lot until we can get all of that extreme buzzing going on in our being down to a manageable state again. For me once I left South Africa and my extreme overworking habits behind, I made a conscious decision to be more present here in my new home country of the UK. I made space and time for nature. I made space and time for my thoughts and feelings. I made space and time for me. This all made such a difference and working less now than I have ever worked in my life, things are just so much better.

Balance has been restored in my little Universe and me and my Soul are happily strolling through life, finding the next adventure at the right time and when it needs to be found. One step at a time.

NOW WHAT?

Our journey to finding ourselves will always be underpinned by judgement. The closer I move to finding more and more about who I am, the more judgement will be showing up. It is my job to recognise that within myself and track it back to a wound and work with it. The more you do this and become aware, the quicker you work with judgement and wounds. Again, it's like riding a bike, we become an expert or a gold medal winner!

The awareness that we carry in ourselves that we are human and that there will always, always be something that triggers us or make us look deeper into ourselves is key.

The more honest you can keep on being with yourself, the easier the journey becomes. The spiral that we are constantly walking brings us back to a new set of treasures within us. And for me that is so exciting.

When I look back over the last 10 years of my 'spiritual' journey I love to see how many things I learnt about myself, about this world, about people and about the Universe out there. It is a never-ending story. And each cycle that I complete and move on from opens up a new cycle.

It also excites me that we as humans have access out there in the vastness of the Universe to so much that we could never even comprehend before. The old ways of being and thinking are slowly crumbling because we dare to be brave and we dare to change our own ways of being within ourselves.

There is a myriad of amazing energies out there waiting to support you and me. These new and beautiful energies that are becoming more seen and more part of our awareness every day have been waiting for ages.

And as I sit here in the warm afternoon sun, feeling my guides peering over my shoulder as I write this, I know that we are all meant to tap into the unknown. The magic lies in all that we have forgotten. And as you dare to live your life each day as if it is an adventure, you see a little more magic and then a little more. Each moment holds a little doorway for you to walk through and to explore.

So remember please, that this journey is not about the hows and the shoulds. It is all about you falling in love with you again. Realising your worth, seeing the potential and the beauty and the amazingness of being a Soul on an incredible planet in the middle of this vast Universe. Stepping out of judgement of yourself. Embracing every weird, quirky, bitchy, sad, happy, ugly, pretty, bad, good part of your human experience.

And every time you catch yourself stepping into that judgement place, ask yourself, 'Is it my shadows that need some attention? Is it my truth that needs to evolve a little more? Is it some wound I need to give some love to? Or do I need to re-evaluate how I want to show up in my power? Do I need to reconnect with trusting my deep knowing again?'

Well, there is a chapter for each of these instances right here in this little book! So head off there, go and tune in again and remind yourself why you can do this!

Remind yourself that you are a glorious creation of the Divine and that you deserve to be here.

You deserve to be heard, to be seen and to be loved.

So go forth and be awesome!

We see you beautiful Starseed Soul!

IN CLOSING

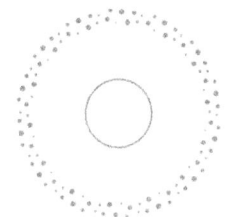

MAGIC

I asked the husband to write me a little piece about how he views our lives and our truths, and this is what he shared with me…

The author and inventor, Arthur C Clarke had this to say on the subject:

> *"Any sufficiently advanced technology is indistinguishable from magic"*

Hi, I'm Rob. Also, probably referred to in this book as "the husband" – although that's mostly accidental. Accidental because our paths happened to cross in a random bar in Lisbon one night. And accidental because, some years after having decided we'd rather like to be together, our son said he'd prefer it if we were actually married. The thing which binds us isn't that simple ceremony, performed on a hillside just outside Cape Town. To put it in Yoli's words, we are the "yin" to each other's "yang" (or maybe it's the other way around – I'm still not very up on the correct mystical terminology).

Where Yolandi's mind sees unicorns and fairies, I see structure, and science and logic. For me, the universe is made up of an array of particles such as quarks, and leptons and bosons. And although I don't necessarily believe in the literal magic which Yoli does (at least not in the same way), I do believe in the magic which Arthur C Clarke understood.

The strange, quantum dance which the fundamental particles of my world perform is just as magical. There's even a word for the strangeness. Because their dance is so rapid and instantaneous, we can never really be sure of their speed or position, so we call it "super position". Super position is the assertion that from an outside view, the particles are everywhere and in every state until we actually measure them. If this sounds vaguely familiar, there's a reason for that. You'll have probably heard of it as the Schrodinger's Cat thought experiment – the cat is both dead and alive until the box is opened, at which point it becomes fixed in one or other of those states.

At this point I'm struggling very hard to not dive ever deeper into the exotic features of my world – there are so many fun ones we could talk about, like quantum entanglement (something even the great Einstein couldn't find better words for than "spooky"). But I really should get to the point before you decide this chapter must also be an accident, and not something which was meant to be in Yoli's book.

What you have just read is a typical weekend morning in our household. We sit in bed drinking our cups of tea, looking at the view from our window, and talking about the universe. Sometimes it's the universe as Yoli sees it, which I don't fully understand but she takes great pains to explain to me in simple terms. And sometimes it's the universe as I see it, which I in return try and explain without all the confusing scientific terms.

My favourite instance of this happened in a hotel in the Cape Town Waterfront. Badly hung over, after a tremendous night of partying with friends, the conversation started with the assertion that we really are all made from stardust. By the time it finished we had gone through the periodic table and the fact that it is widely believed that some of the particles inside us (gold for example) can only be created in massively powerful cosmological events such as supernova (exploding stars).

If, like me, your mind tends towards the scientific, you will recognise the last two paragraphs as some of the accepted wisdom of how our universe works. You may argue some of the details, but the overall arc is the framework which today's science offers us to explain our existence. But it is important to understand that is all it is – one explanation of our existence. And it's not a very precise or complete one at that. Even if we ignore quantum entanglement (which I'm still resisting the urge to get into), there's a couple of parts that we can't yet explain.

For now, we have just given them the labels of 'dark matter' and 'dark energy' but these are not some minor details needing to be tidied up in an otherwise perfect model. These account for most of the matter in the universe, and its expansion for the last 13.8 billion years since the Big Bang. In times past there have been many other attempts at explaining our existence. In the times of the druids, for example, terms like 'sorcery' or 'alchemy' might have been used for the things they couldn't explain or understand yet.

What's important to realise is that those of us following science are not standing on some firm foundation of bedrock from which we can render all other explanations as weird bunkum. Our explanation is just as poorly formed and, in all likelihood, the real explanation for how the universe really works will probably be far stranger than any of us can imagine. And until we have that full, proper understanding it's fine to believe in your own magic, whether yours is the yin or the yang.

Written by Rob Walker (aka the husband)

EPILOGUE

I never thought I would actually write a book, but at last here we are and you got to the end of this one. It has been one of the most amazing experiences of my life and I can totally recommend the process of ripping your insides out and examining them bit by bit, to everyone out there. Questioning yourself, working through your truths and evaluating your own judgement is a bit of a game changer.

And all this because of a dream five months ago, whilst visiting my parents in South Africa for my Dad's 70th birthday. Running out of my room early morning, to find a pen and piece of paper, hearing my Dad ask if I am okay and me shouting, 'Yes, but I need to write this down before I forget. I just had a crazy dream about writing a book…'

In my dream (and you are allowed to laugh out loud here cause I am still laughing my head off when I think about it) my ex-best friend, Rebecca Campbell, Kyle Gray and some hot guy with long hair all met me in a little tiny restaurant with very little space to sit. Rebecca (I don't actually know her btw but am a huge fan) started lecturing me about what to do and to write (not that I can remember any of it, but she spoke a lot). Kyle (also don't know him) was very quiet in the corner and hot guy with long hair just tagged along. My ex-best friend was going on about repatriating dogs from Spain (I still don't know what that means). So we enjoyed a lovely lunch and then all headed out to a limousine and a helicopter but more than that, I can't remember. I remember waking up and knowing what the book needed to be about and that gave me a starting point.

But what I love is how it evolved and how it grew into something that I did not foresee. To be honest, I am happy about what she, my dear book, wanted to share with you and I hope you can take something from our time together and implement it in your own life. I also hope that this has opened some new rabbit holes for you to go and dive into and explore. Somehow bringing you closer to your own truth.

We each have a choice, and that is all this life is, a series of choices. And none of it is right or wrong, always know this. Your heart is here for you to navigate by, but sometimes we forget and sometimes it is just too damn hard, and that is okay. One step at a time. Be gentle and be kind to yourself, we are all only human!

So much love and blessings

Yolandi xxxx

ACKNOWLEDGEMENTS

To my dearest husband Rob, you will never really understand how much I needed you to step into my life, so thanks for choosing to email me that very first time and for pursuing this connection of ours. You are my world and I love you so much. Your support of all my weirdness and this strange world that I spend so much of my time in is epic. And to Ben, thanks for your amazing wisdom, my boy. You make me want to be myself more and more each day. I love you with all of my being.

To my Mom and Dad, you rock and thanks for always being there, no matter how strange things got. Your love and support will always live in my heart.

To Lameze, thanks so much for being my book doula and for the countless hours of forest walks, sea staring and voice notes. I love you and thanks for always being there.

To Nicola, thanks for taking a chance on my idea, and for all the support and love. You and your entire team are amazing and I am proud to be a part of the Unbound family.

To Nicole Cienne (www.nicolecienne.com) thanks for my gorgeous photos. You captured my Goddessness!

To my Gridkeepers Crew, love you guys madly. To Leche, thanks for the reading reassurance babe. To all my friends and clients who were forever checking in on me and making sure I was doing this thing, you know who you are and I love you for being in my life!

And to my dear Soul, thanks for being such a force within and for always having my human back.

ABOUT THE AUTHOR

Yolandi is a lightworker, spiritual coach, teacher and healer, with a passion for travel, sacred sites and spiritual adventure.

She teaches clients from more than 35 countries across the world how to listen to their inner guidance and return to the essence of their Divine Souls. She does this through DNA Activations, Light Language Healings, Akashic Record Readings, Soul Channelling and Coaching. She also shares her teachings through her podcast, YouTube channel, group meditations, workshops and retreats.

You can find more information about working directly with Yolandi on **www.divinesoul.me**

www.ingramcontent.com/pod-product-compliance
Lightning Source LLC
Chambersburg PA
CBHW071729080526
44588CB00013B/1952